ACCIDENT HANDBOOK

The **Practical Guide** to
Louisiana Personal Injury
Law for Car Wreck Victims

Copyright © 2015 by Parker Layrisson

All rights reserved. No part of this book may be used or reproduced in any manner whatsoever without written permission from the author.

Printed in the United States of America.

ISBN: 978-0-692-47247-7

Published by:

HF Group
1010 N Sycamore Street
North Manchester, IN 46962

ACCIDENT HANDBOOK

The **Practical Guide** to Louisiana Personal Injury Law for Car Wreck Victims

Parker Layrisson

www.AccidentHandbook.com

To my incredible parents, Eddie and Celeste Layrisson.

You have always supported me.
This book would not be possible without you.
Thank you for your guidance, example, and encouragement.
I love you.

છે

Advance Praise for
ACCIDENT HANDBOOK

"I had the privilege to read an advance copy of Parker Layrisson's *Accident Handbook*. It was written as a helpful guide to a person involved in the litigation process, but, because it is so comprehensive, and so readable, I recommend it to lawyers who handle these sorts of cases.

Mr. Layrisson not only covers the basic issues in this sort of litigation in great detail—liability of the defendant, causation of the injury, and damages, he also carefully addresses ALL of the innumerable problem areas which invariably arise, and that many lawyers fail to consider: dealing with health insurers, interventions, subrogation issues, insurance coverage issues, workers compensation issues and many others.

I will keep this book on my desk."

Edward J. Walters, Jr.
Attorney at Law – Baton Rouge, LA

"The modern legal system is convoluted even for 'simple car crash cases.' Parker's book is a thorough guide that patiently explains everything that a auto accident victim should know about how their case will be handled: from dealing with insurance adjusters, to hiring the right lawyer, to dealing with car repairs. Parker's book is an exceptionally well-crafted guide for anyone injured in an auto accident."

Ernest Svenson
Attorney at Law – New Orleans, LA

"The insurance companies have armies of adjusters and lawyers to do everything they can to deny claims. Parker's book is the sling every accident victim should have in their arsenal to take on Goliath."
Robert L. Campbell
Attorney at Law – Baton Rouge, LA

"Parker does a great job of simplifying the complex world of personal injury law in a practical and straightforward manner. *Accident Handbook* is complete and thorough, and offers practical advice to those who need it most during frustrating, stressful, and confusing times. And not only is it a resource to the layperson, but a well-researched guide for seasoned practitioners."
Christopher K. Jones
Attorney at Law – Baton Rouge, LA

"I've known Parker some many years and believe him to be a fierce advocate for his clients while at the same time being available and compassionate to those he represents. *Accident Handbook* is very much a reflection of both his detail-oriented approach and accessibility. It conveys with great detail the nuances of an auto accident dispute and, at the same, is easy to read and understand."
Ravi Sangisetty
Attorney at Law – New Orleans, LA

"I keep Parker's book in my right hand drawer of my law office desk, and I refer to it often. It is not only a great reference book for those seeking help with his or her own auto accidents needs, but also for fellow lawyers who know and admire Parker's depth of knowledge in this area of law."
J. Christopher Zainey, Jr.
Attorney at Law – New Orleans, LA

"Parker is always going above and beyond for his clients. *Accident Handbook* is the latest example of Parker spending countless hours to better serve his clients and to provide them with the best information and representation. *Accident Handbook* will surely be a valuable resource for his clients and many others."

Robert J. Landry – Houma, LA
Attorney at Law

"As an advocate, Parker always goes the extra mile to ensure his clients get the best representation possible. *Accident Handbook* is further evidence of Parker's dedication to his clients and his expertise in an area of law that proves difficult for many lawyers. This book is by far the best personal injury resource out there."

Blair B. Alford – Covington, LA
Attorney at Law

"A practical guide written for real people, not lawyers, that explains the entire process from accident to settlement of an auto accident case in plain English. Clients will never have to worry about what comes next in their case because this book will be their guide. Even if you don't hire Parker, auto injury victims can use this book to make sure that their attorney is doing what they should be doing."

Andrew Legrand – New Orleans, LA
Attorney at Law

Contents

PREFACE

Dedication
Advance Praise
Table of Contents
Disclaimer
Introduction

PART I: AUTO ACCIDENT BASICS

1. How to Determine If You Have a Good Case 1
2. Top 10 Auto Accident Myths 3
3. How to Protect Yourself After an Accident 5
4. What to Expect During Your Case 7
5. 7 Simple Steps to Fix Your Car 17
6. Top 5 Mistakes That Can Wreck Your Claim 23
7. What an Attorney Can Do for You 31
8. What an Attorney Should Cost 35
9. 5 Easy Steps for Choosing the Right Attorney 39
10. Attorney-Client Privilege and Confidentiality 51
11. Handling Your Case Without a Lawyer 53
12. Length of Claim and Litigation 55
13. Settlements Are a Good Thing 57
14. The Most Important Advice 63

PART II: LOUISIANA PERSONAL INJURY LAW

15. Recovery of Damages 67
16. What You Must Prove to Win Your Case 93
17. Presumptions of Fault 103
18. Beware of Social Media 107
19. Time Limitations 109
20. Insurance Coverage 111
21. Mediation and Arbitration 119
22. The Discovery Process 137
23. Wrongful Death and Survival Claims 143
24. Liens and the Like 147
25. Intentional Torts 161

PART III: MEDICAL MATTERS

26. Common Traumatic Injuries 173
27. Health Care Treatment Options 185
28. Medical Mistakes to Avoid 197
29. Independent Medical Examination 203

PART IV: COMMERCIAL CONCERNS

30. Commercial Truck Accidents 209
31. Employer Liability 227
32. Workers' Compensation 239
33. Products Liability 245

APPENDIX: LEGAL LAGNIAPPE

Frequently Asked Questions 257
Louisiana Lawyer's Oath 283
Louisiana Rules of Professional Conduct
    1.2. Representation 285
    1.5. Fees 287
    1.8. Conflicts of Interest 291
    1.15. Safekeeping of Property 299
Acknowledgments 305
About the Author 309
Why We're Different 311
Rave Reviews from Our Clients 317
Testimonials from Other Attorneys 321
Contact Information 323
Incredible Free Offer 325

Disclaimer

No Legal Advice, Attorney-Client Relationship, or Guarantee

Although this book was written by an attorney, it is not legal advice or solicitation of legal services. The material included here is intended solely for general educational and informational purposes, and it is not intended to create, and its receipt does not constitute, any attorney-client relationship. Absent an express written agreement between you and J. Parker Layrisson, L.L.C. (d/b/a Parker Layrisson Law Firm) executed by Parker Layrisson, no attorney-client relationship will be established. The author disclaims all liability regarding actions taken or not taken based on any contents of this book. You should not act upon the information presented here without first seeking professional counsel. Each case is different, laws change frequently, and an attorney can only give you quality legal advice when he or she understands the exact facts involved in your case. The author is not a medical doctor and has not received any medical or chiropractic training. With regards to any medical conditions discussed in this book, defer to the opinions and advice of a licensed health care provider. Also, no lawyer can guarantee or warrant the outcome or result of any case or matter. Past results do not guarantee future success. If you may have a legal claim, contact an experienced attorney immediately. Strict deadlines may apply that require prompt action. The author does not state or imply that he or any attorney affiliated with the Parker Layrisson Law Firm are "experts," "specialists," "certified," "board certified," "better," or "best." Finally, it is not the purpose of this guide to compare our lawyers to other attorneys.

Introduction

If you were injured in a car wreck, you have probably already asked yourself these questions:

- Who will pay my medical bills?
- Do I have a good case?
- How can I protect my rights?
- Should I talk to the insurance adjuster?
- What are the worst mistakes to avoid?
- How long will this take?
- Do I need a lawyer?
- How much does a lawyer cost?
- How do I choose the right lawyer?
- Will I have to go to court?
- How much is my case worth?

Most accident victims seek straightforward answers. Before you talk to insurance adjusters, sign any forms, or hire the wrong lawyer, you deserve reliable information you can trust.

Unfortunately, instead of offering helpful straight talk and practical guidance, many personal injury lawyers take advantage of car accident victims with sleazy "your pain is my gain" TV advertising and high-pressure "sign with me right now" sales tactics. It is difficult to know whom you can trust.

Making matters worse, it's an unfair fight. A giant insurance company stands between you and a reasonable recovery. Allstate, State

Farm, GEICO, and other huge insurance companies do this every day. They know personal injury law inside and out. They are experts at avoiding responsibility for accident-related injuries. Insurance companies often try to confuse you, or even intimidate you, and beat you down so that you cannot recover what you are legally entitled to receive. They have hundreds of defense lawyers on call. They have the tools to determine exactly what they owe you, and they know the tricks to get out of paying you a fair settlement. Do not expect the insurance companies to treat you fairly if you fail to fight for your rights.

This is a modern day David-versus-Goliath situation.

Like David, you need a great plan and the right tools to succeed in defeating the giant who stands in your way. Instead of a sling and stones, you need dependable information and (possibly) an experienced personal injury attorney. What you really need is a trusted partner who understands personal injury law—someone to educate you about this situation and stand up to the insurance company. You may need a respected advocate to hold that company accountable and protect your rights. At the very least, you need a knowledgeable advisor to help you make good decisions.

That's why I have written *Accident Handbook*. As a personal injury lawyer, I help clients injured in car accidents recover the compensation they deserve, without needless frustration and stress, even if they have no money to pay me or their doctors. But in that profession my influence is limited to my actual clients (fewer than 100 cases per year). On the other hand, as an author, I can expand my reach to help you and countless others who need practical guidance. Through this book, I can share with you warnings about the top mistakes to avoid, as well as practical "insider info" that could help you maximize your financial recovery and minimize your stress levels.

This guide answers the most common questions that accident victims like you ask personal injury lawyers like me. It offers tons of information to help you make the best and most-educated decisions about what you should do next.

You can review this helpful information in the comfort of your own home, at your individual pace, whenever you like. Knowledge is power, and *Accident Handbook* will empower you with the guidance and understanding you need to stand up to the auto insurance company positioned between you and a fair settlement.

Use this book to determine your next step. It will help you identify and avoid the "land mines" hidden throughout the complicated personal injury claims process. This information will help you decide if you have a good case and whether you need a lawyer to protect your rights. If you decide to retain an attorney, this guide can help you find the right one—an experienced advocate who will do the following for you:

- Answer all your questions and guide you through the complicated claims process;
- Collect and organize the information and documents you need to build your case;
- Force the insurance companies to play by the rules and treat you fairly; and
- Help you get the money you need to recover and move forward—with less stress!

Good luck!

PART I:
AUTO ACCIDENT BASICS

CHAPTER 1
How to Determine If You Have a Good Case

If you have been seriously injured in an auto accident, you may have a valuable claim. An experienced personal injury lawyer could help you maximize your financial recovery. However, not every injury resulting from a motor vehicle crash is worth money. Within a few months of your accident, you should discuss the following questions with an attorney:

1. Was the accident someone else's fault?

If someone other than you caused the crash, you may have a winnable case. However, if your careless driving was the sole cause of the accident, financial recovery is highly unlikely.

2. Was there visible damage to your vehicle?

Although major property damage is not absolutely necessary to a successful personal injury case, photos of auto damage are helpful to proving your case. Judges and juries are more likely to believe severe injuries were caused by an accident when supported by evidence of moderate to high vehicle impact.

3. Were your injuries promptly treated by a doctor?

Injuries and medical treatment are essential to a successful auto accident injury claim. Thus, it is important to determine that soon after your wreck you sought medical attention from your family doctor, chiropractor, emergency room, or walk-in clinic. Moreover, your case value depends on whether you followed your health care providers' recommended course of treatment.

4. Did your accident occur less than a year ago?

In Louisiana, personal injury lawsuits such as auto accident claims must be filed within a year of the accident. Therefore, if more than a year has elapsed since your crash and you have not yet filed suit, it may be impossible to succeed in your claim.

5. Is liability or uninsured motorist (UM) insurance available to cover your claim?

No matter how severe your property damage and injuries, if the driver who caused your collision has no money or insurance and you do not carry UM insurance, your claim could be worthless. As the old saying goes, "You can't bleed a turnip."

If your accident was someone else's fault, your vehicle damage was noticeable, your injuries were promptly and properly treated, your accident happened less than a year ago, and adequate insurance coverage exists, you probably have a good auto accident case. Each case is different, so contact a lawyer to discuss your case in more detail.

CHAPTER 2
Top 10 Auto Accident Myths

The following myths cause many false assumptions about Louisiana car wreck claims:

- **Myth #1:** An auto accident settlement will make you rich.

- **Myth #2:** If you write the insurance company a reasonable settlement demand letter, you will get a reasonable settlement offer in return.

- **Myth #3:** You must give the at-fault driver's insurance company a recorded statement and sign their forms, or they won't settle with you.

- **Myth #4:** The insurance company for the at-fault driver is obligated to pay your medical bills as they are incurred.

- **Myth #5:** If you make a claim for uninsured motorist (UM) insurance benefits, your insurance rates will skyrocket.

- **Myth #6:** All lawyers who advertise that they handle auto accident or personal injury cases have the same abilities, resources, and experience to handle your case.

- **Myth #7:** You cannot afford to hire an attorney to handle your case because the up-front fees and costs are too high.

- **Myth #8:** Because you have been involved in an accident that was not your fault, there must be some insurance funds available that will pay for your medical bills, lost wages, and pain and suffering.

- **Myth #9:** You can expect the same settlement your friend, brother, neighbor, co-worker, etc., got in an accident case with similar injuries.

- **Myth #10:** Louisiana juries are generous.

CHAPTER 3
How to Protect Yourself After an Accident

There are several simple steps you can take to protect your rights after a motor vehicle accident:

- Get medical treatment.
- Preserve accident and injury evidence.
- Refuse to talk to the other driver's insurance adjuster.
- Contact a personal injury lawyer.

Under Louisiana law, any person whose fault causes you harm is liable to pay for your damages. This means that if a reckless driver caused a car accident that resulted in your injuries, then that driver must repair your vehicle, pay your medical bills, replace your lost wages, cover your out-of-pocket expenses, and compensate you for your physical and mental pain and suffering, among other things. Where the other driver's automobile insurance or other liability insurance applies, insurance companies employ claims adjusters. They are trained risk management professionals who represent the insurance companies' interests—not yours!

First and foremost, you should attend to your injuries by seeking immediate medical attention from a doctor. Go to an emergency room, family practice, after-hours clinic, chiropractor, or other licensed health care provider. Thereafter, follow your doctor's advice about follow-up treatment and go to every scheduled medical appointment. Injuries must be proven through medical records and expert testimony; it is not enough for you to say you are hurt. Also, you should collect all of the information you can from accident witnesses and other drivers, including names, addresses, license plate numbers, telephone numbers, insurance info, etc., as well as police info. Save all the documents you receive that relate to the accident and your injuries: accident reports; photos of the accident scene, your vehicle, and your injuries; names and contact information of witnesses; medical reports; medical bills; and receipts for prescriptions, vehicle repairs, and other related out-of-pocket expenses. Damages must be proven with actual evidence; the insurance company will not believe your word without supporting documentation.

> **FAST FACT**
> Lawyers charge contingent fees in personal injury cases, meaning that you do not pay anything up front and the lawyers do not get paid until you get paid.

Additionally, you should refrain from discussing the details of the accident or your injuries with anyone except the police, your doctors, and your lawyer. Do not count on insurance adjusters who call you on the telephone to deal fairly or protect your rights in any way. Think of the usual line from police movies: "Anything you say can and will be used against you in a court of law." Although you are not a criminal, the same principle applies: loose lips sink ships! Adjusters and other witnesses can twist your words and use them against you later on. Therefore, do not give a statement to the other driver's insurance adjuster. Also, do not sign any insurance company forms.

Finally, if you have been injured in an automobile accident through no fault of your own, you should contact a Louisiana personal injury attorney for a free consultation. Lawyers typically charge a contingent fee in personal injury cases, meaning that you do not pay anything up front and the lawyers do not get paid until you get paid by settlement or judgment.

CHAPTER 4
What to Expect During Your Case

Your personal injury attorney should maximize your financial recovery and minimize your stress. A big part of minimizing your stress is preparing you for what to expect during the case. Although every case is different, there should not be many major surprises if your lawyer is keeping you well-informed from the start.

You should begin by asking your lawyer what to expect. Focus on specifics. This book shares how I handle expectations with my own personal injury clients in order to demonstrate what you should expect.

> **FAST FACT**
> Your personal injury attorney should maximize your financial recovery and minimize your stress.

For example, on Day 1 of every case, I let my clients know that I will handle the hassle of the insurance claims process so that they will not have to face a giant insurance company on their own. This conversation includes details of how I will use my personal injury law experience to level the playing field between my clients and the giant insurance companies standing in their way. From the outset, my clients understand that they can count on me to do the following:

- Answer all their questions and guide them throughout this difficult process.
- Collect and organize the information and documents we need to build their case.

- Force the insurance companies to play by the rules and treat them fairly.
- Help them get the money they need to recover and move forward.

If you were my client, in addition to detailed meetings and telephone calls discussing our plan, I would follow up with a letter such as this one to remind you of what to expect during your case.

Dear Client,

Allow me to share some information about what to expect during the handling of your personal injury case. This letter explains how our process works at the Parker Layrisson Law Firm. It is a general overview that outlines the four major phases of your case:

1. Medical Treatment;
2. Investigation;
3. Settlement Negotiations; and
4. Litigation.

Please feel free to call or email me with any questions about specifics. It is important to me that you are informed throughout this process.

Each case is different. We will custom-tailor our representation to fit your exact needs. However, over a decade of experience handling personal injury cases has taught us that the following "blueprint" usually provides our best plan for maximizing your financial recovery and minimizing your stress levels.

PHASE 1: MEDICAL TREATMENT

Successful personal injury cases begin with prompt and thorough medical treatment. It is important to see a doctor soon after the accident, and to tell your physician about each and every part of your body that you believe you injured in the accident, no matter how minor you may believe the injury is at the time. Often, mild post-accident pain will worsen with time, later revealing a severe and perhaps permanent injury caused by the accident. This is especially common in spine injuries involving the neck and back.

In addition to telling your doctor about everything that physically hurts after the accident and all related emotional and mental problems, you should also report any missed work or trouble performing routine activities. Follow your physician's advice faithfully and return to the doctor as often as recommended or as often as necessary. It's important that you maintain consistent medical treatment—a minimum of one visit per month—until you are released from your doctor's care. It is also critical that you keep my team informed of your treatment status.

Complete and accurate doctor reports are crucial to the successful handling of your claims. Ideally, your doctors' reports will do the following:

- *Set forth all of your injuries and symptoms;*
- *Describe your pain and suffering;*
- *Relate your injuries, symptoms, and treatment to the accident; and*
- *Express an opinion on any future problems, treatment, restrictions, and disability.*

Medical billing is a major concern for most of our clients. If you have health insurance, such as Blue Cross Blue Shield, you should have that company pay for as many of your medical costs as possible (this could save you a lot of money). Car insurance medical payments coverage is another helpful form of payment. In some cases, our law firm will either advance payment for your treatment or guarantee payment on your behalf. These decisions are made on a case-by-case basis that require further discussion as your medical treatment progresses.

PHASE 2: INVESTIGATION

First, upon accepting any case for representation, we go into fact-gathering investigation mode. This means you will be working directly with members of my team to make sure that our law firm has access to all the relevant information that is available about you.

Usually, we will need five or more years of your pre-accident medical records, employment wage information, photographs, and all post-accident medical reports and bills. We will also need copies of your driver's license, auto insurance card, and health insurance card (if applicable). To assist us in gathering this information, will ask you to complete and return a detailed client questionnaire outlining your confidential personal information, medical history, and litigation/claims experience. It asks for most of the information we expect the insurance company to request from you as the case goes on.

It will be your job to work closely with my team to make sure that we don't miss anything. During this initial phase, I may be the last person in the office to actually "know" some details about your case. Instead, my team of highly-trained law clerks, case managers, paralegals, and assistants will be contacting you from time to time with questions as we learn and document more about you and your case. It is important that my team knows everything we can in order to help you best.

In addition to contacting you, we will be gathering information from the police, witnesses, insurance carriers, medical providers, and other potential witnesses. The fact-finding investigation process typically lasts months. Its exact length depends on the duration of your medical treatment and a few other factors.

PHASE 3: SETTLEMENT NEGOTIATIONS

Once your medical treatment ends, you reach maximum medical improvement, and other conditions are met, we will prepare a confidential detailed settlement evaluation for your case and share it with you. (By the way, we are serious about this settlement evaluation being confidential. Please don't share it with anyone except your most trusted "advisors" and, by all means, do not make a copy of it and give it to anyone.) It contains the "path to success" for your case.

This is where I become more intimately involved in your case. My team will schedule a meeting or telephone call between you and me for the purpose of determining whether we are "on the same page" with regard to the value of your case before settlement negotiations begin. We will invest a great deal of knowledge and analysis into your detailed settlement evaluation. I will personally share my input about the value of your case.

The confidential evaluation will contain information about your past and present medical condition and any future care that will be predicted by your physicians. We'll tell you what we know about the medical bills, any liens or unpaid bills, your lost wages and, in particular, we will tell you what we know about your prior claims (if any), and much more data that we think is important to your case.

I will then apply my many years of experience handling Louisiana accident injury cases to give you a good idea about the settlement value of your case. I will help you make the best possible financial decision about your case. Our valuation will be based not only on our own cases and trial experience, but also upon our "quantum study" legal research review of literally thousands of cases over the years, our discussions with insurance claim adjusters, other lawyers, and judges, and attendance at advanced continuing legal education seminars for accident injury attorneys.

> **FAST FACT**
> ••••••••••••••••••••••••••••••
> We will negotiate with the insurance company until we have what we believe to be their "top offer" before trial.

Your job when you receive the confidential settlement evaluation is to consider it very carefully and help my team "fill in the gaps." There may be information about your life that we may have missed or that you, your doctors, or your employer may have forgotten to tell us. It will be important for you to help us complete the settlement evaluation so that we are all on the same page about the facts of your case.

When we meet, either by phone or in person, you and I will discuss our settlement strategy. You will consider granting me your authority to settle your case. It may be as simple as you saying, "Parker, go ahead and try to settle my case per your recommendations for an amount you deem fair based on your years of experience handling similar cases." On the other hand, you may prefer to set a specific "bottom-line number" for settlement authority. Sometimes you will want to discuss either a higher or lower value of your case. Many clients never want to go to trial, and it is important, if you share that preference for avoiding trial, that we know that before we start the settlement negotiations. We need to know whether you prefer to fight for top dollar all the way to trial or to settle at all costs before trial.

We will not begin negotiations with the insurance adjuster until we have your full authority to do so and until you and I are on the same page regarding settlement of your case. We will then prepare a written "settlement demand" to send to the insurance company. That package will have our analysis and supporting documentation.

Although you and I certainly will have discussed the "soft spots" in your case, our settlement demand to the insurance company will put the case in the light most favorable to you. It will also typically suggest a much higher settlement payment than we expect the insurance company to approve. Generally, you should not get your hopes up that they will pay anything nearly as high as we initially request.

During settlement negotiations, we will communicate to you all the settlement offers from the insurance company, and we will help you "do the math" to let you know the amount of money you will net in your pocket if the case settles at the current offer. We will negotiate with the insurance company until we have what we believe to be their "top offer" before trial. This may or may not be an offer that you want to accept, but it will be your decision after discussing the offer with us.

The most commonly known way to recover personal damages is to sue that party in the court of law through a process called litigation (discussed below). However, because of the risks and delays inherent to litigation, we will often suggest a form of Alternative Dispute Resolution (ADR) to assist in reaching a settlement. ADR is a general term encompassing various techniques for resolving conflict outside of court using a neutral third party. Our favorite form of ADR for personal injury claims such as yours is mediation.

> **FAST FACT**
> It is your decision (not your lawyer's) whether to accept the insurance company's offer.

Mediation is a non-binding method of ADR where a neutral third party called a mediator facilitates communication between opposing parties, such as you and the insurance company, in the effort to promote a mutual agreement on how to resolve the case.

The mediator's job is to be a neutral third party who helps guide negotiations and settlement between the parties. In many cases, a mediator will be able to help you and the defendants decide on a mutually agreeable amount of damages to be paid without having to bring the case to trial. If the mediation process does not work—if you and the defendants are not able to agree on a settlement—you still have the option of litigating the matter in court. The mediator cannot make you do anything you do not agree to do.

We will often continue negotiations right up to trial. Even after the lawsuit is filed, settlement is possible. Indeed, many cases settle just before trial (or even once trial begins!). However, remember that if we go to court, we will have large additional expenses such as paying your treating doctors to testify, which could result in a smaller net recovery for you.

PHASE 4: LITIGATION

If your case cannot be settled by agreement with the insurance company, we will file a lawsuit on your behalf. At that point, you officially become a "Plaintiff." After we file the lawsuit, called a "Petition" or "Complaint," the court will serve a copy of it to the driver and insurance company we sued, called "Defendants". They will then have a certain amount of time to file an answer to the lawsuit. The answer usually denies most allegations of the lawsuit.

The pre-trial portion of litigation begins with a formal investigation process called "Discovery." Discovery is the legal term for the compulsory disclosure of information at the request of an opposing party. It allows all parties to learn more about the facts of the case by interviewing witnesses and obtaining evidence. Usually it involves formal written questions called "Interrogatories," written evidentiary requests called "Request for Production of Documents," authorizations for the release of various types of medical, employment, and financial records, and a process for obtaining your sworn statements under oath called a "Deposition." Again, my team will be involved in much of the underlying work and trading of information with the insurance defense attorneys in the pre-trial stage of your case. They are highly trained at helping you answer discovery requests, scheduling depositions, and otherwise preparing the case for trial.

After the discovery portion of litigation ends, if a settlement cannot be reached, the case goes to trial in front of a judge (called bench trial) or jury of laypersons (called a jury trial). At that time we will present evidence, witnesses, and interpretation of the facts and events that unfolded surrounding your accident and resulting damages. The judge or jury will decide the outcome of the case, including who was at fault, to what extent they were at fault, and what amount of damages, if any, should be awarded to you.

> **FAST FACT**
> Trial can be very lengthy and expensive for both sides.

This process of taking a case to trial can be very lengthy and expensive for both sides, sometimes taking years to resolve the matter. This means, even if we win at trial, it could be years before you receive any actual money from the insurance company and driver who caused your accident and injuries.

Most cases like yours are resolved before trial. Indeed, over 95% of our firm's personal injury cases settle before appearing in court for trial by judge or jury. However, beginning the day you hire us, we prepare your case for trial against all odds because that is the best way to earn top value for your case.

If the case goes to trial, I will be the principal trial lawyer on your case and all strategic decisions will be made by me. I may engage another lawyer to assist me with trial (at no extra cost to you).

Once trial ends, one or more parties may appeal the trial court's verdict. To appeal means to apply to a higher court for a reversal of the decision of a lower court. In Louisiana, the Circuit Court of Appeal reviews the decisions of the District Court (trial court). All lower court decisions are subject to the oversight of the Louisiana Supreme Court. In some instances, the United States Supreme Court provides the final word, although such cases are exceedingly rare. The practical upshot of appeals is that the process can take years and delay your recovery even if you prevail.

ANY QUESTIONS?

If at any time during this process you need to speak to me, it is as simple as calling the office and setting up a specific appointment for a phone call, in-person meeting, or virtual meeting. If I'm not in trial or out of town on depositions, an appointment can usually be made to speak to me within 72 hours. It is important to me that you understand this process. I'll do whatever it takes to keep you informed.

> **FAST FACT**
> Before hiring a lawyer, ask for a "blueprint" of what to expect.

Sincerely yours,

J. Parker Layrisson
Attorney at Law

CHAPTER 5
7 Simple Steps to Fix Your Car

Car crash claims can be costly and confusing. Almost every auto accident involves a trip to the body shop. From a basic busted bumper to total loss requiring a rental car, your property damage claim requires the prompt attention of the responsible insurance company. Unfortunately, what to do and whom to talk to in order to get your vehicle repaired or replaced can be confusing. Making matters worse, your situation is probably urgent. Every day we need our cars to travel to and from home, work, school, etc.

> **FAST FACT**
> You can probably handle your own car repair claims without involving a lawyer.

As an auto accident personal injury attorney, I have helped countless clients handle their property damage settlements (at absolutely no cost). However, almost all accident victims are able to handle their own car repair claims without a lawyer. Here are seven simple steps to recover for your property damage on your own.

1. Document the Damage

At the scene of the wreck, take as many pictures as possible. Your cell phone probably has a decent camera—use it. Immediately after the accident is a great time to visually document your property damage before information about the collision is lost. It is also a good idea to record the accident scene and your immediate recollection of what occurred, since details of the accident are often later forgotten or disputed. Your cell phone video camera can be especially helpful as you document the following details:

- Date and time of the accident
- Location of the accident
- Position of the vehicles
- Damage to the vehicles
- Traffic signs, obstructions, point of collision, etc.
- Immediate recollection of the details of the accident

2. Obtain Information and Police Report

In addition to documenting your damages, it is important to gather the following contact information from the people involved in the accident: names, addresses, telephone numbers, driver's license numbers, insurance companies, insurance policy numbers, and more. Ask to photograph their driver's licenses and proof of insurance cards. If the owners of any vehicle were not involved in the accident, it is important to gather their information as well.

If a police officer investigated the accident, a police crash report should become available within 5–10 business days. It is typically a good idea to call police to the accident scene because the police report can be extremely helpful to proving your case. It is therefore important to obtain the police report as soon as possible. To that end, be sure to record the name of the investigating police agency and officer. Finally, if your vehicle must be towed, tell the tow company where you would like it to be taken or make sure to collect the information about where they are taking it.

3. Notify Insurance Companies of Claim

The next step is contacting the at-fault driver's insurance company to make a claim for your property damage. This company's identity should be listed in the police report. The contact information for their claims department should be available online (*e.g.*, Google "State Farm Auto Claims"). Be aware that any conversations with any insurance companies could be recorded and whatever you say can be used against you to deny your claims for property damage and personal injuries. For this reason, it is important to be careful and consistent in your statements. Remember, insurance adjusters are trained professionals who may twist your words against you to minimize your recovery. Therefore, if you have serious injuries, you should probably ask your attorney to participate in any talks with insurance adjusters.

In addition to contacting the at-fault driver's insurance company, you should consider contacting your own insurance agent to make your claim for property damage. The upside of this path is that your insurer will likely pay you more quickly than the other driver's company; the downside is that you may be required to pay a deductible, although it should later be refunded. Your insurance company can reimburse you for the damage and then seek to recover those costs from the other company through a reimbursement process called subrogation.

4. Get a Body Shop Estimate

As soon as possible, get a repair estimate from the body shop of your choosing. Do not wait idly by for the insurance company to give you the cost to repair your vehicle or rely solely on their appraiser's estimate for the amount of damages. Although many people do not do this, it is always a good idea to get your own independent estimate from an auto shop you trust. It is best to bring it to the shop that you plan to have perform the repairs to receive the most accurate estimate of your costs.

Although it can be more convenient and is perfectly okay to use the insurance company's approved auto shop, know that it is up to you where you bring your car, not the insurance company. Also, request an estimate for factory replacement parts, not used parts, and make sure the estimate is as detailed as possible and includes all costs such as paint, parts, and required labor. The more detailed the estimate, the easier it will be to justify the amount requested.

If the estimated cost to repair your vehicle is greater than the value of the vehicle, then an insurance company should deem the car "totaled." Indeed, insurance companies typically consider a car to be totaled once the cost of repairs reach 75% of its value. The insurance company will pay you the value of the vehicle prior to the accident, minus the salvage value (the cost that it could be sold for as scrap). Although a body shop may not be able to estimate the value of your totaled vehicle, it is still important that a trusted auto shop give you a proper estimate for repair to aid in this determination.

5. Submit Your Claim in Writing

Once you have received the police report, repair estimate, and any other property damage costs, you should provide them to the insurance company by email, fax, and/or certified mail (submitted in writing). It is important to be able to prove when the estimate was actually sent to the insurance company. In order to do this, you should document as to when and how you provided your proof of claim to the insurance company. For example, if mailed, you should request a certified mail return receipt that lets you know when the mail was received. If faxed, then make sure to save the fax confirmation sheet for safekeeping, and if emailed make sure to request and preserve a notice that the email was received and read.

6. Calendar the 30-Day Bad Faith Deadline

The reason for proving the date you submit the repair estimate is Louisiana's bad faith law. If an insurance company does not pay your property damage claim within a certain period of time—30 days—the insurance company may be found to be in bad faith. If they are in bad faith, the insurer may be required to pay additional amounts of money as a penalty for their undue delay. This is why it is extremely important to document when and how your estimate and request for damages was delivered to the insurance company.

In Louisiana, an insurance company can be subject to a bad faith claim if they fail to pay an undisputed claim within 30 days of the proof of property loss. A valid repair estimate can be considered proof of property loss, so this means the insurance company must pay your repair estimate or give a reason why they are disputing the amount within 30 days of receiving it. Although an insurance company is allowed a few exceptions for issues such as time needed to investigate the claim, they are not allowed an unreasonable delay in making payments without cause. Therefore, it is important to document when your estimate was sent and keep the 30-day rule in mind when asking for payment from an insurance company. Although it likely will require hiring a qualified auto accident attorney to recover these additional bad faith damages, it is important to know they are available when an insurance company delays payment in bad faith.

7. Avoid Insurance Adjuster Tricks & Traps

First and foremost, if you suffered any bodily injury as a result of the accident, do not sign anything without legal advice. Allow a Louisiana personal injury lawyer to review any documents first. It is important that you double-check accuracy and avoid waiving your bodily injury claims and any other rights unrelated to property damage. Often times when you accept payment on your property damage claim, the insurance company may ask that you not only waive your right to further property damage claims, but personal injury claims as well. Always be aware what rights you are waiving. If you have been hurt in an accident, even slightly, it is always a good idea to consult an attorney first. Handling your own property damage claim is not a complicated process, but asking an attorney when in doubt is never a bad idea, especially when signing documents or waiving rights you do not understand.

Also, insurance companies routinely underestimate the cost of repairs and try to pay less than you ask for, so make sure you are fully compensated for your repairs (or at least to your full satisfaction). If you later find additional work that needs to be done, you will not be able to recover for this cost after signing the release form. Remember, you are in a negotiation with the insurance company. Their objective is to pay you the least that they can, so make sure your numbers are well researched and don't accept less than you should. However, if you follow these seven simple steps, you will be on the right track to fixing your vehicle as soon as possible.

CHAPTER 6
Top 5 Mistakes That Can Wreck Your Claim

Mistake #1: Not Getting Enough Information at the Accident Scene

Failure to preserve evidence at the scene of the crash can doom your auto accident case before it begins. This can be avoided with two simple steps: 1) call the police; and 2) collect information yourself.

Often, accident victims are reluctant to call the police to investigate after their collisions. They are afraid it will waste their precious time and cause their already high auto insurance rates to skyrocket. I understand their temptation to leave the police out of it. However, without the police officer's prompt and (usually) thorough investigation of the accident scene, it becomes much more difficult to prove an accident injury case. Police officers document car crash evidence and make an initial determination of fault. Although they make mistakes, of course, police are more often than not correct in their reporting. While police reports are not the final say on fault (they are not binding in court), they carry tremendous weight with insurance adjusters towards establishing liability (responsibility for the accident). Moreover, police officers interview witnesses and obtain contact and insurance information from the relevant parties and witnesses. In short, involving the police can help you win your case.

> **FAST FACT**
> Preserve evidence at the scene of the crash and call the police immediately.

23

In addition to contacting the police, there is helpful information you can collect on your own. Begin by getting contact information, driver's license number, and license plate number from the at-fault driver. Also, get the names, phone numbers, and addresses of any eyewitnesses at the scene. This is important because sometimes witnesses leave the scene before the police arrive. If possible, photograph the accident scene and vehicles as well. This could show where and how the accident occurred and verify the damage done. If your mobile phone does not include a camera, keep a disposable camera in your glove box—just in case! Remember, once the scene is cleared and debris is removed, the accident site can never again be exactly duplicated.

Mistake #2: Giving a Recorded Statement to the Other Side's Insurance Company

There is little reward and much risk in giving the other driver's insurance company a recorded statement. As mentioned above, we usually advise clients to avoid discussing accident or injury details with anyone except police officers, doctors, and lawyers—especially insurance adjusters. Adjusters are trained professionals skilled at obtaining harmful statements that will understate your injuries and minimize the other driver's fault in causing the accident. While they often pretend to be friendly resources "at your service," they work for the insurance company, not you! Remember: "Anything you say can and will be used against you in a court of law."

A better idea than speaking directly to the insurance adjuster to give a recorded statement is to allow your lawyer to do the talking for you. Like the adjuster, your auto accident attorney is an experienced professional who knows which statements will help or harm your case. You are far more likely to harm your case by conversing with an adjuster than by allowing your lawyer to speak on your behalf. Moreover, your attorney's statements on your behalf are not potentially admissible at trial like your own statements. In short, your attorney can harmlessly give the insurance adjuster all the information needed to settle your claim without requiring you to submit a potentially harmful recorded statement.

If you prefer to represent yourself and insist on giving a recorded statement to the insurance company, keep it short and simple. If possible, describe the accident in one short sentence (*e.g.*, "I was rear-ended while stopped at a traffic light facing east on Government Street in Baton Rouge."). Likewise, do not discuss your injuries in detail. Instead (assuming this is true), briefly state that you were injured in the accident and are treating with medical professionals as a result (*e.g.*, "I injured my back and neck in the accident, and I'm treating with Dr. Jones as a result."). Do not let the adjuster trick you into stating that the accident was your fault or that the injuries were caused by an event other than the collision.

Mistake #3: Waiting Too Long to See a Doctor

If you have been injured, seek medical attention as soon as possible after your auto accident. Perhaps the worst mistake you can make to wreck your auto accident injury case is to avoid or delay medical treatment. You should, of course, see the health care provider of your own choosing: emergency room, urgent care clinic, after-hours clinic, family doctor, orthopedist, neurologist, chiropractor, etc. Just do not wait until it is too late.

In all auto accident injury cases, physical injuries must be proven through medical records and expert testimony. Insurance companies will not "take your word for it" if you simply say you are hurt because of the accident and nevertheless neglect to treat with a doctor. Without medical evidence from a licensed health care provider, the insurance company will say that you are not hurt or will argue that you were injured by a cause other than the motor vehicle accident. They will not pay you for your injuries unless you prove the existence and cause of your injuries with medical evidence. Treating yourself with home remedies and over-the-counter medications such as aspirin or ibuprofen is not enough. Your doctor's examination, diagnosis, prognosis, plan of treatment, and expert opinion on causation are necessary to prove accident-related injuries worthy of compensation by the insurance company.

Not only is it necessary for your case to obtain medical treatment, it is imperative that you see a doctor as soon as possible after the accident. The longer you wait after your accident to seek treatment, the more likely the insurance company will deny payment of your claim based on their argument that the collision did not cause your symptoms (and the more likely it is that a judge or jury will buy that argument). Although medical science proves otherwise, some people will not believe a legitimate auto accident injury can arise days, weeks, or months after the accident. This creates a problem of proof for procrastinators and "tough" clients who avoid the doctor's office despite actual accident injuries. It is also a great reason to get checked out by a doctor after your accident, even if your symptoms are minor.

> **FAST FACT**
> If you have been injured in an accident, go see a doctor as soon as possible.

Often, especially with neck and back injuries, symptoms worsen weeks or even months after the accident that caused the harm. It is not unusual for auto accident victims to initially "tough it out" and endure injury symptoms for months without medical treatment, only to find that the problem gets worse with time. By the time they discover serious and permanent issues causing their pain, like herniated or bulging spinal discs, it is too late to put together a successful insurance claim to pay for the necessary treatment, pain, and suffering. Therefore, if you have any pain, stiffness, soreness, aches, or other symptoms following a motor vehicle accident—small or large—see a doctor at once. It's better to be safe than sorry.

Mistake #4: Waiting Too Long to Hire a Lawyer

Just as delaying your visit to the doctor can doom your claim, waiting too long to hire an auto accident attorney can wreck your case. Nobody knows better what you must do to succeed in your case than an experienced lawyer. An attorney's guidance can be critical to avoiding major mistakes and achieving maximum settlement or judgment value.

Beyond wise counsel, attorneys are capable of essential action. Your lawyers will begin by investigating the facts of the case and educating you about the auto accident claims process. They will promptly contact insurance companies to initiate claims on your behalf while stopping insurers from directly contacting you. They can obtain the police report, insurance policy information, medical records and bills, photographs, and other evidence you need to prevail, and share it with the insurance company. They can interview accident witnesses, police officers, and health care providers, all the while recognizing and analyzing any legal issues that come along. Of course, they will decide if and when you should file a lawsuit and handle that litigation from start to finish, spotting potential problems and anticipating the insurance company's defenses in the process.

These are but a few of the many important tasks your lawyers can accomplish on your behalf. The earlier you hire experienced auto accident attorneys, the sooner you can adopt a smart game plan for your claim and take appropriate action. You will avoid major mistakes while making the right moves to protect your rights.

Mistake #5: Lying About Accidents, Injuries, Income, or Activity Levels

Once you begin a case, the insurance company will be interested in knowing how many past accidents you have been involved in. The reality is that they probably already know the answer or have easy access to that information. All insurance companies subscribe to insurance databases and often the only reason they ask you this question is to test your credibility. If you have been in other accidents, your lawyer can investigate this and make a determination as to whether this is a valid problem in your case or not. However, if you do not tell your lawyer about the other accidents, and you misrepresent your accident history to the insurance company, then it is highly likely that you will lose or significantly damage your case.

You should be up-front and honest with your attorney about any injuries that occurred before or after this accident. If you saw a doctor or other health care provider, then there is a record in existence that the insurance company will find. Your lawyer can deal with this if he or she knows about it. However, if you lie about it, and the insurance company finds out, then your case is likely doomed.

In many cases, claimants will have lost income because of their accidents. You will only be able to claim your lost income if your past tax returns are truthful and accurate. You don't want to risk going to jail by claiming a loss of income, only to have your past tax returns not back up your claim. Also, if you are exposed for lying about lost wages, it is highly unlikely the judge or jury will believe you about any other issues. Again, being honest with your attorney is the only way to be, because he or she can then deal with the problem and advise you on the appropriate course of action.

Finally, insurance companies routinely hire private investigators to conduct video surveillance. If you claim that you cannot exercise, dance, run, lift, or play with your kids, and you get caught on videotape participating in those activities, your claim will be doomed. Many clients are foolish enough to lie about their activity levels to the insurance company and their lawyer, only to be exposed by insurance company private investigators who tape surveillance video. Don't make the same mistake.

> **FAST FACT**
> If you lie about your injuries or activities, you will doom your case.

CHAPTER 7
What an Attorney Can Do For You

Your personal injury attorney should maximize your financial recovery and minimize your stress. Your lawyer should handle the hassle of the insurance claims process. He or she should protect your rights every step of the way, even if the odds are stacked in favor of giant insurance companies like Allstate, State Farm, and GEICO. Your attorney should do this by using his or her personal injury law experience to level the playing field between you and the Goliath insurance company standing in your way.

> **FAST FACT**
> Your lawyer should maximize your financial recovery and minimize your stress.

If you ask my personal injury clients what our team does for them, they will probably focus on the following aspects of our services:

- We answer all their questions and guide them through this difficult process.
- We collect and organize the information and documents we need to build their case.
- We force the insurance companies to play by the rules and treat them fairly.
- We help them get the money they need to recover and move forward.

Your lawyer should perform many tasks to handle your car crash injury claim. Each case is different and, depending on the facts involved, not all actions listed below will be necessary or possible in every case. Nevertheless, here is a brief list of some—but not nearly all—of the functions an experienced auto accident attorney may be able to accomplish on your behalf:

- Investigate the facts of the case.
- Educate the client about the auto accident claim process.
- Contact insurance companies to initiate claims on the client's behalf.
- Stop insurance companies from directly contacting the client.
- Obtain the police accident report, insurance policy information, medical records and bills, photographs, and other evidence.
- Review and analyze automobile, medical payments, uninsured motorists, umbrella, and health insurance policies to see whether there is any coverage available to pay for the client's damages.
- Recommend any necessary changes to the client's insurance policies to ensure future protection.
- Interview accident witnesses, police officers, health care providers, etc.
- Recognize and analyze legal issues such as tort liability, comparative fault, liens, subrogation, etc.
- Obtain narrative reports from treating doctors to help explain the client's medical condition and determine its cause.
- Determine whether any money spent by insurers, Medicare, Medicaid, etc., to pay the client's medical bills must be repaid under the law out of the recovery.
- Decide if and when to file a lawsuit.
- Propound discovery by drafting Interrogatories, Requests for Production of Documents, Subpoenas *Duces Tecum*, and Requests for Admissions.
- Respond to opposing counsel's Interrogatories, Requests for Production of Documents, and Requests for Admissions.
- Depose defendants, health care providers, and other witnesses.
- Prepare the client for deposition and defend the client at deposition.
- Conference with the court and other counsel.

- File any necessary motions and supportive memoranda with the court and argue motions before the judge in open court.
- File briefs in opposition to the defendant's motions and oppose their motions in open court.
- Request the case be set for trial.
- Schedule the case for mediation or settlement conference.
- Prepare the client and other witnesses to testify at trial.
- Organize and prepare medical records, exhibits, and demonstrative aids for trial.
- Try the client's case before a judge or jury.
- Analyze the judge or jury's verdict to determine if an appeal is necessary and likely to succeed.

As stated above, this list of personal injury attorney services is not exhaustive. In fact, the basic checklist of attorney tasks I have developed to guide our firm in handling each personal injury case is ten pages long! These services are just a few of the many provided by experienced attorneys.

CHAPTER 8
What an Attorney Should Cost

Legal services are not a commodity that you should shop for based purely on price. Rarely is the cheapest lawyer the best attorney available. Hiring a lawyer based solely on fee rates is almost as foolish as representing yourself. Instead of bargain shopping for the least expensive lawyer possible, you should carefully compare available attorneys in an effort to hire the most capable lawyer you can afford.

To put the matter in perspective, imagine that you need an important medical procedure, such as neck surgery. Would you rush to hire the cheapest available physician without checking the doctor's credentials as a practicing spine surgeon? Of course not! With your health on the line, you would research your options carefully to ensure that you hired a respected professional with solid qualifications. You would select someone who focuses on that specific field of practice—a doctor with excellent spine surgery training, related experience, and a proven record of success. In short, you would hire the best doctor you could afford, the surgeon who would give you the best chance of success.

> **FAST FACT**
> Personal injury lawyers require no up-front money from the client. Instead, we charge a percentage of the eventual settlement or judgment collected, typically 33%–40%.

Like neck surgery, your legal issue probably deals in high stakes. Therefore, you should be as careful selecting the most qualified attorney available as you would in choosing a surgeon. Any short-run savings derived from hiring the least expensive attorney available (or worse, representing yourself) could be dwarfed by the larger long-term costs of inadequate representation. Hire the most accomplished lawyer you can afford—the attorney who will give you prepared, precise, and effective legal services. You will not regret it.

There is no denying the fact that legal services are costly. Effective representation typically comes at a steep, but reasonable, price. Like buying a home or hiring a surgeon, retaining an effective attorney is expensive, important, and ultimately valuable if you make the right choice. However, lawyers should always inform you up front, in writing, as to how they will bill you for their services.

In general, attorneys usually charge clients through one of the following standard payment arrangements:

1. Hourly rate fee,
2. Flat fee, or
3. Contingent fee.

The hourly rate fee is the most common payment method. Under this arrangement, the attorney charges an agreed-upon hourly rate for all time spent working on a client's case until it is resolved. Hourly rates vary based on attorneys' experience, expertise, prestige, operating expenses, and the local market. Nationally, lawyers' hourly rates range from as little as $100 to as much as $1,000. Here in Louisiana, most attorneys charge anywhere from $150 to $450 at the time of this writing. Paralegals' services are also billed under this method, at a lower rate.

Hourly rate fee agreements typically require the client to pay the attorney an advance payment called an advanced deposit or retainer. Usually, the lawyer deposits that payment into a special bank account, called the IOLTA client trust account, and deducts from that account the cost of services as fees accrue. For example, a local divorce lawyer may charge $200 per hour while requiring at least $4,000 to be paid up-front.

Less common than the hourly rate fee is the flat fee arrangement, which is usually reserved for relatively straightforward, predictable, and well-defined matters such as wills, contracts, uncontested divorces, basic bankruptcies, and some criminal defense matters. Under this arrangement, the attorney and client agree upon a fixed amount of payment. For example, the flat fee for a basic will might be $500, while a DWI defense flat fee could be $5,000, regardless of the time the lawyer ultimately takes to complete the matters.

> **FAST FACT**
> Under the contingent fee arrangement, attorneys' fees are only paid fees if a favorable result is achieved.

In certain types of cases, such as the car accident personal injury and wrongful death cases I handle, lawyers work on a contingent fee basis. Under this arrangement, attorneys' fees are only paid if a favorable result is achieved (*i.e.*, "no win, no fee"). This means that the lawyer requires no up-front money from the client, but instead the attorney gets a percentage of the eventual recovery—typically 33%–40% of any settlement or judgment collected.

The contingent fee arrangement provides access to the courts for victims of others' fault who cannot otherwise afford to pay attorneys' fees. Contingent fees also provide a powerful motivation for attorneys to work diligently with a results-oriented emphasis. This form of fee arrangement is typical for plaintiffs in injury claims, medical malpractice cases, debt collection matters, and select commercial cases. However, contingent fees are legally prohibited in criminal and family law disputes.

Under the hourly rate fee, flat fee, and contingent fee models, in addition to payment of attorneys' fees, lawyers require reimbursement of any out-of-pocket case-related expenses (such as court costs, filing fees, postage, court reporter bills, copies, mileage, etc.) regardless of the fee model utilized. Clients are not, however, billed for attorneys' general overhead expenses.

Given that attorneys' fees are typically high but ultimately reasonable, use your understanding of the various arrangements for payment to negotiate a written fee agreement that best suits your needs. Get it in writing—ALWAYS!

CHAPTER 9
5 Easy Steps for Choosing the Right Attorney

The single most important decision you can make in handling your injury case is choosing the right attorney. Put simply, a bad lawyer can ruin your case. That could result in real tragedy.

Not all attorneys are created equal. The right lawyer could be the difference between winning and losing.

Time is of the essence. In car accident cases, the clock begins to tick on important legal deadlines right away, so you must decide on whom to hire in a hurry.

Nevertheless, you can make a smart, informed decision quickly if you use common sense and follow a few straightforward guidelines:

- Do your homework
- Examine experience
- Question qualifications
- Research reputation
- Interview attorneys

Begin by considering the importance of hiring a good lawyer. This will motivate you to put in the work necessary to finding the right attorney. When dealing with the law, the stakes are high. Auto accident injury cases put your health and wealth on the line. You deserve legal protection provided by an effective, experienced lawyer whom you can trust. If you do not take a moment to consider how much you have riding on the outcome of your case, you will never commit to doing the work necessary to selecting the right lawyer.

Do Your Homework

Once you appreciate the significance of hiring the right lawyer, the first step is "doing your homework." With any important decision in life—buying a home, choosing a career, hiring a doctor or lawyer—you will make a better decision if you carefully investigate your options. There is no reason to put less effort into choosing your lawyer than you would to pick out your next automobile or smartphone. Study your options carefully. It's important.

The quickest and easiest place to begin is the internet. The obvious upside of an online search is that it allows 24-7 access to a tremendous amount of information about the law and lawyers. However, there is such a thing as internet information overload, a fact you may observe when your search turns up an abundance of self-serving hype by "lazy lawyers" who are more interested in their financial bottom line than your legal needs. You must be especially suspicious of lawyers' ads and law firm websites that promise to "be aggressive" and "care about you." Remember, no lawyers (even "lazy lawyers") look bad on their own websites!

> **FAST FACT**
> You shouldn't put less effort into choosing your lawyer than you do into buying your next smartphone.

The best way to balance the abundance of the web's online information with its potential negative effects is to supplement your internet search through word-of-mouth investigation, written information requests, and attorney-client interviews.

As discussed below, the most important considerations in selecting the right lawyer are:

- Experience
- Qualifications
- Reputation

Websites, legal directories, publications, friends, attorneys, and many other sources can provide you with this information. However, while each of those sources can be helpful and informative, none is ultimately as effective as speaking to the attorneys directly. Most attorneys will talk to you by phone about the legal issue you are facing and, if they handle the type of case you have, will typically offer to meet with you in-person. This initial meeting is called a consultation. You should use this opportunity to interview attorneys and confirm who the best fit is for you.

However, before you schedule your first attorney interview, you should conduct some advance research at home. This will help you "weed out" any obviously bad fits.

Ultimately, investigating your options up-front could save you time and energy. A few minutes of smart online research could prevent hours of meetings with lawyers who are patently wrong for your case. It could also prevent you from overexposing yourself to the awkward "sales" situation created when lawyers try to pressure you into hiring their firms during a consultation.

Before you set up consultations with any attorneys, ask the lawyers you are considering to send you written information through the mail or email. Specifically, request the following:

- A written outline or explanation of the process involved in your type of case;

- A professional biography or curriculum vitae that summarizes the lawyer's qualifications and experience;
- A sample fee agreement that outlines the fees and costs the lawyer will charge you; and
- A written confirmation of professional responsibility insurance (legal malpractice coverage) of at least one million dollars.

If any lawyers refuse or fail to produce these basic materials upon request BEFORE you meet with them, watch out!

Examine Experience

Experience is incredibly important. Hiring a "green" lawyer could be disastrous. Do not assume all attorneys have the experience necessary to handle your case properly. Not all lawyers have "paid their dues," obtaining the quality experience you need.

The first aspect of experience to consider is the length of each lawyer's legal career. In general, you should probably avoid rookie lawyers if you can afford a more experienced attorney. However, do not focus exclusively on how many years the attorneys have practiced law; question them about what they have been doing all those years. With regard to experience, quality is as important as quantity.

Next, you should examine the focus of attorney experience. For example, if you need an injury lawyer, determine how many similar injury cases the attorneys have handled, how many of those cases went to trial or settled, what results were achieved in those cases, etc.

Another aspect of experience worth exploring is employment

history. Some prior jobs prove particularly helpful in preparing lawyers to handle certain types of cases. For example, if you have a criminal defense case, you should consider hiring a former prosecutor or public defender who has worked in that jurisdiction. If your matter is pending in a certain court, ask whether any of the attorneys have clerked for that judge.

Experience matters. The following is a list of helpful questions addressing experience that you should consider asking any attorneys you interview:

- How long have you been a practicing attorney?
- How long have you been practicing in auto accident personal injury law?
- How many cases of this type have you handled?
- How successful have you been at trial?
- How successful have you been at settlement negotiations?
- What percentage of your caseload is focused on auto accident personal injury law?
- What previous employment best prepared you to handle my case?
- Have you clerked for a judge or worked for other government officials?
- If so, would your past work in the public sector or other law firms help to handle my case?

Question Qualifications

Every lawyer licensed to practice in Louisiana is technically "qualified" to handle your case. However, you should demand much more than this basic "qualification" in your attorney. Do not settle for the bare minimum.

Begin by considering intelligence. It will benefit you greatly if your lawyer is "the smartest person in the room" during trial and negotiations. Although IQ is difficult to measure, law school grades nevertheless provide valuable insight into attorneys' intellectual capacity and legal analysis skills. Intelligence is just one of many qualifications to consider, but it is extremely important.

Publications are another window into attorneys' capabilities. Ask lawyers whether they have published any articles, reports, or books. Materials written about your type of case can help you determine whether your expectations align with an attorney's approach. Moreover, authors are typically respected as "thought leaders" and authorities.

Additional aspects to address are manner and appearance. Your attorney should be well-spoken with a professional demeanor. Regarding appearance, begin by verifying that the lawyers you are interviewing have quality websites. An impressive online presence is important in this day and age. Next, check out their office space. Is it clean and professional? Finally, analyze the personal appearance of the attorneys and their support staff. They need not be physically attractive, but their looks should be professional and appropriate. Your lawyer's image should command respect.

When you hire a lawyer, you actually engage a law firm of legal professionals and support staff. For this reason, you should ask about the entire team of partners, associates, and staff. Who will answer and return your phone calls and emails? Will the lawyer handling your initial consultation appear at all hearings and meetings, or will a separate associate attorney be assigned? In short, take a moment to analyze the entire team, not just the lead lawyer.

Finally, a key qualification to consider is community involvement. The best lawyers serve both the legal industry and the community at large in leadership positions. Within the legal field, ask about participation in bar associations, Inns of Court, and other lawyer groups. Also, check to see if the attorneys have taught continuing legal education (CLE) courses for other attorneys and judges. Look for lawyers who have helped the greater community through non-legal civic groups. Top lawyers serve society through service organizations like Rotary, Kiwanis, and Jaycees, as well as PTAs, nonprofits, and public boards. You should hire an attorney who has not only participated in organizations as a member, but has led these groups as an officer elected by his or her fellow members. Serving as president or treasurer of a community organization demonstrates that this lawyer has earned public trust.

The following questions about qualifications will help you interview attorneys for your case:

- Where did you go to school?
- What were your grades?
- Have you continued your education in the area of law applicable to my case?
- Are you active with any law journals, bar associations, or professional groups?
- Are you a community leader? Explain.
- Have others trusted you with authority in community organizations (*e.g.*, club officers, boards of directors, youth sports coaching, etc.)?
- Do you have a professional website that describes your qualifications?
- Have you been selected by well-respected legal organizations to lecture on auto accident personal injury law?
- Have you been selected by your peers to lead bar associations, Inns of Court, law reviews, legal journals, and other lawyer organizations?

- Have you written any books, articles, or other publications? If so, please provide a copy.
- Do you have an experienced, knowledgeable, informative, and courteous team working with you on every case?
- (Ask Yourself) Are the attorneys well-spoken with appropriate personal appearances?
- (Ask Yourself) Do you feel comfortable with the attorneys and their staff?
- (Ask Yourself) Do the attorneys work out of professional-looking offices?

Research Reputation

This topic can be awkward to address and difficult to evaluate, but it nevertheless remains extremely important. Your lawyer's reputation could be critical to your success. Do not assume the lawyers you interview are widely respected. Rather, investigate their reputations via industry insiders, online legal directories, social media, word of mouth, awards, and actual client testimonials.

> **FAST FACT**
> The most respected and popular legal directories are Martindale-Hubbell®, Avvo®, and Super Lawyers®.

If you have access to judges, court reporters, bailiffs, or even other lawyers, bluntly ask them what they think of the attorneys you are considering to handle your case. This "courthouse gang" of local insiders would know better than most people which lawyers are the most capable.

Online legal directories are another excellent reputation resource. The most respected and popular directories are Martindale-Hubbell®, Avvo®, and Super Lawyers®. Unlike some less reputable sources, ratings in these directories are earned rather than purchased.

Perhaps the most credible source of this type is the Martindale-Hubbell® Peer Review Ratings™ system available at www.martindale.com. At over 130 years old, Martindale-Hubbell®'s system is the trusted "granddaddy" of attorney ratings services. Moreover, due to its system of obtaining anonymous ratings from peer attorneys and judges, this directory provides a fairly objective indicator of a lawyer's ethical standards and professional abilities. Ratings are based on attorneys' legal knowledge, analytical capabilities, judgment, communication ability, and legal experience. Ideally, you should hire a lawyer rated AV Preeminent® by Martindale because this rating reflects an attorney recognized by judges and other lawyers as having achieved the height of professional excellence in legal ability and ethical standards.

Martindale-Hubbell® also provides client review ratings that allow actual clients to provide feedback on attorneys and evaluate their services. Martindale's system asks clients questions that assess communication ability, quality of service, responsiveness and value for the money on matters for which they engaged the lawyers.

If Martindale-Hubbell® is the gray-bearded veteran of lawyer review services, Avvo®.com is the scrappy up-and-comer. Since 2007, Avvo® (short for *avvacato*, the Italian word for lawyer) has grown to become the world's largest legal directory. It claims to rate over 95% of American lawyers. Avvo® rates lawyers on a numerical scale from 1-10, with 10.0 Superb being the highest rating available. The Avvo® rating is calculated using a mathematical model that considers the information shown in a lawyer's profile, including a lawyer's years in practice, disciplinary history, professional achievements and industry recognition—all factors that, in Avvo®'s opinion, are relevant to assessing a lawyer's qualifications. Avvo® claims its method can help you find the right lawyer because it's unbiased and easy to understand.

Another popular lawyer rating service is Super Lawyers®. With a selection process patented by the United States Patent and Trademark Office, Super Lawyers® selects its attorneys using peer nominations combined with third-party research. Each candidate is evaluated on 12 indicators of peer recognition and professional achievement. Selections are made on an annual, state-by-state basis. Less than 5% of Louisiana attorneys make the Super Lawyers® list, and less than half of that total make the Super Lawyers® Rising Stars list of exceptional lawyers under the age of 40. These lists are available at www.superlawyers.com.

In addition to online legal directories, the internet provides tremendous resources for reading reviews of attorneys by their clients. The two most popular places should be no surprise: Google and Facebook. Google is constantly improving its local services. Part of this process has been the evolution of Google+ Local, which allows people to review local businesses and other places they visit using a 5-star scale and comments. Facebook also rates local businesses using a 5-star scale and comments. For all lawyers and law firms that you are considering, check out their reviews on Google and Facebook. These online services are a great source of modern word-of-mouth information.

Awards are another indicator of a good reputation. With awards, it is important to consider the source and verify that the awards are not "for sale." For example, some advertisers, like the telephone book, reportedly offer their advertising customers "awards" only if they purchase certain advertisements. Beware of "awards" that are for sale; these are a scam. A few awards you can trust are Martindale's "Client Distinction Award" and Avvo®'s "Client Choice Award." They are earned through superior ratings from real clients, not bought.

Finally, client testimonials are perhaps the best source of reputation information. In addition to online reviews of attorneys by former clients, you should ask the lawyers you interview for copies of client satisfaction reviews, quotes, and other testimonials.

To research reputation, consider the following questions:

- (Ask Others) Do the attorneys have reputations for success in the city and parish where you need help?
- (Ask Others) Do the attorneys have statewide reputations?
- (Ask Others) Do the attorneys have national reputations?
- (Check Online) Do the attorneys have AV Preeminent® ratings on Martindale.com?
- (Check Online) Do the attorneys have 10.0 Superb ratings on Avvo®.com?
- (Check Online) Are the attorneys listed as Super Lawyers or Risings Stars on SuperLawyers.com?
- (Check Online) Do the attorneys have 5-star ratings on Google and Facebook?
- (Ask Around) Do judges, other lawyers, court reporters, bailiffs, and other "insiders" recommend the attorneys?

If you choose to engage in a telephone or in-person consultation with a particular attorney after you have conducted this research, be sure to ask him or her the following questions:

- Do you receive referrals from other Louisiana attorneys? If so, from whom?
- Do you receive referrals from prior clients? If so, from whom?
- Do you receive referrals from other professionals such as doctors, engineers, CPAs, etc.? If so, from whom?
- Can you provide testimonials from prior clients?
- Have you won any awards for client satisfaction or legal service? If so, please provide copies.

Interview Attorneys

Once you request, receive, and review the written materials discussed above, it is time to consult the top lawyers on your list. This is perhaps the most important step in hiring the right attorney. This "initial consultation" process is important because it allows you to determine whether you like and trust the lawyers, and it permits the attorneys to decide whether they want to handle your case. Use this time to conduct a thoughtful interview.

> **FAST FACT**
> The most important considerations in selecting the right lawyer are experience, qualifications, and reputation.

Accomplished lawyers will welcome your questions because they will take it as a sign that you have done your homework. It shows the attorneys that you take your case (and their job) very seriously. Remember that when you are interviewing an attorney, that lawyer is also interviewing you to see if he or she wants to take your case. A good lawyer would rather represent a truly prepared client—that is, a client who is committed to getting the best legal representation available.

If you dedicate yourself to a thorough attorney-client interview focusing on the lawyer's experience, qualifications, and professional reputation, your chances of choosing the right lawyer for your case will increase tremendously. Therefore, you should not be afraid to interrogate the lawyers regarding these topics. Ask thoughtful, direct questions. Demand straight answers. Consider the information you obtain, and go with your instincts. It is important to be both comfortable with and confident in your attorney.

CHAPTER 10
Attorney-Client Privilege and Confidentiality

One question that crosses the mind of nearly every client or potential client I meet is, "Can I trust my lawyer to keep our conversations confidential?" The answer, in a word, is "yes." While clients often value attorneys for qualities such as aggressiveness, intelligence, and creativity, loyalty is our profession's most essential attribute. Through the concept of attorney-client privilege, lawyers are required to keep client communications confidential and are protected from being forced to reveal client secrets.

Attorney-client privilege, which goes back to the days of Elizabethan England, is one of the oldest recognized privileges for confidential communications. It encourages clients to speak openly and honestly to their lawyers, who are then better able to provide effective legal representation. The privilege is indispensable to attorneys' function as advocates because lawyers can only properly prepare cases with the benefit of full and frank client disclosure.

To invoke attorney-client privilege, you only need to communicate with your attorney for the purpose of securing legal advice. There are, of course, exceptions to the privilege. The most common are:

1. Communications made in the presence of non-clients,
2. Communications made in furtherance of a crime, and
3. Waiver by client's public disclosure of communications.

Attorney-client privilege applies even after a lawyer no longer represents you. Attorneys who breach the privilege can be reprimanded or even disbarred. Airing clients' dirty laundry is considered a breach of fiduciary duty. Therefore, feel free to trust your lawyer to keep your conversations confidential. The attorney-client privilege will protect your privacy.

CHAPTER 11
Handling Your Case Without a Lawyer

Many car wreck injury claims can be fairly settled without involving attorneys. For example, minor injuries requiring less than three months' medical treatment with bills less than $3,000 are often settled directly between the accident victim and insurance company. Although I recommend that you consult a lawyer to discuss your case because each case is different and strict legal filing deadlines may apply, I recognize that not every accident victim will do that, especially in very small cases with limited damages.

> **FAST FACT**
> You might not need a lawyer.

If you insist on negotiating directly with the insurance company without the assistance of an attorney, proceed carefully and demand that the insurance company answer the following questions before you give a statement or sign any forms:

1. Will you put in writing that the accident was not my fault?
2. Will you put in writing how much insurance the person who hit me has, including umbrella coverage?
3. If I agree to give a recorded statement, will you first give me a copy of any recorded statement(s) you have already obtained from the person(s) who caused the accident?
4. If I sign the medical record release, will you immediately forward to me a copy of everything you receive by using my release?
5. Will you give me copies of the recorded statements that you have taken from any witnesses?

6. Will you tell me in writing whether you have already done video surveillance of me?
7. Will you put in writing whether the driver who caused the accident was in the course and scope of any employment at the time of the accident?
8. Will you put in writing whether the driver who caused the accident was covered by any other insurance coverage, including umbrella coverage?
9. Will you give me a copy of any financial information that you may have already obtained on me?

If the insurance company will not answer these questions **before** you give a statement or sign any forms, look out!

If your attempts to settle your own injury claims are unsuccessful, you should contact a Louisiana auto accident injury attorney for a consultation within six months or less of your accident date. Involving an experienced lawyer will "level the playing field" between you and the insurance adjusters who negotiate these claims for a living.

CHAPTER 12
Length of Claim and Litigation

Predicting the length of litigation is difficult. Each case is unique. A host of factors outside your control could expedite or delay the process. Some cases settle quickly, while others last for years, awaiting trial and appeals.

For example, in my law practice I have handled matters decided by trials within a week of the initial disputes. On the other hand, I have tried cases so old they were filed by other lawyers more than a decade before I arrived on the case! However, most lawsuits fall somewhere between those stark extremes.

Usually your attorney will spend months attempting to settle your case before filing a lawsuit. Once litigation is filed, lawyers will conduct pre-trial discovery, an investigatory process that could take years to complete. It begins with formal written requests for information and evidence, followed by depositions where attorneys question witnesses under oath before court reporters. Another common pre-trial activity is mediation, a meeting between the parties and a neutral mediator designed to facilitate a final settlement. Once trial is set in civil matters, it can last anywhere from a few hours to a few months depending on the complexity of the case and the size of the court's docket.

> **FAST FACT**
> Some cases settle quickly while others last for years, awaiting trial and appeals.

Of course, trial is not necessarily the end of litigation. Parties have the right to appeal the trial verdict. Appeals can take even longer than trial court proceedings.

Considering the delays inherent to trial and appellate litigation, estimating your case length is tough. As a general rule, you can expect simple disputes to move faster than complex cases. Considering the uncertainty of trials and appeals alongside the fact that settlements always produce prompter results, as a party to litigation you should ask yourself whether "a bird in the hand is worth two in the bush."

CHAPTER 13
Settlements are a Good Thing

Many people have the wrong idea about personal injury settlements. They do not like the idea of settling their claims because they believe that a settlement means accepting less than they deserve. Also, some injured auto accident victims falsely believe that hiring a lawyer means they cannot or should not accept a settlement offer before trial.

As a result, many personal injury claimants foolishly reject reasonable settlement offers made by insurance companies prior to trial. They hold out for "top dollar" and take their case to trial before a judge or jury, only to be disappointed when their eventual recovery is delayed or denied.

I am not suggesting you consider accepting a "lowball" offer from the insurance company. Lowball offers are unreasonable settlement offers designed to prey upon accident injury victims' ignorance and desperation. For example, if the insurance company offers you only a few thousand dollars before carefully analyzing your medical records and bills, that is a patently unacceptable lowball offer. If, after months of ignoring your calls, the insurance company calls during the holiday season with a small "Christmas cash" offer, that too is a lowball offer. Unfortunately, most offers made before you hire a lawyer—and many even after your attorney begins negotiating—are lowball offers.

> **FAST FACT**
> Lowball offers are unreasonable settlement offers designed to prey upon accident injury victims' ignorance, hardship, and desperation.

Nevertheless, as long as you avoid unreasonable lowball offers, the truth is that most of the time personal injury settlements are a good thing. That is why well over 95% of all auto accident personal injury cases result in a settlement rather than a trial. The benefits of settling your case within the fair market value verified by your personal injury attorney far outweigh the risks associated with gambling on a trial.

Settlements do not represent "settling for less." Rather, settling just means that you and the defendant have reached an agreement that ends the lawsuit on terms that both of you can live with. Louisiana law has recognized this fact for centuries. Indeed, our Civil Code calls a settlement agreement between parties a "compromise."

Settling your case outside of court, without a trial and appeals, will result in much faster payment for your damages. Often, cases that fail to settle can take years to get to trial before a judge or jury. These delays can be lengthened for additional years by the appeals process. Some cases that fail to settle do not pay out for decades. A settlement will shorten the recovery time frame. If you have significant bills to pay out of your personal injury case recovery, that's a big deal.

Settlements can also result in more money in your pocket. First, they can do this by removing the risk of a costly loss at trial or a low verdict in your favor. Also, settlements save on court costs, such as expert witness fees, that can run thousands of dollars per hour in some instances. Some fee agreements call for your fees to go up if your case reaches a lawsuit, trial, or appeals, so settling before then could possibly save you legal fees as well.

Finally, settlements can reduce your stress by allowing you to control the outcome with a "sure thing" rather than risking it all by "rolling the dice" on the uncertainty of a trial verdict. There are always big risks with trial. Appeals are also risky. Judges and (especially) juries can be quite unpredictable.

Timing is critical when it comes to entering into settlement negotiations. Your personal injury attorney should have a well-planned strategy for maximizing your financial recovery via settlement. (Don't expect me to share settlement strategies here. It's too easy for insurance defense lawyers to get a copy of this book!) Your settlement strategy will surely require completion of medical diagnosis and treatment planning, as well as additional fact gathering.

> **FAST FACT**
> Most of the time personal injury settlements are a good thing.

Before your attorney negotiates your settlement with the insurance company, he or she should take all the time you need to carefully explain the process and obtain your express authority to enter settlement negotiations. Your lawyer should inform you of any and all offers made by the defendants, unless you agree otherwise. All settlement demands and counter-offers made on your behalf should also be subject to your approval. Your lawyer cannot settle your case without your permission.

Every personal injury claim is different, so the settlement value of each case is different. Your attorney should discuss with you in depth what your case is worth and the different factors that go into evaluating a case for settlement. For example, the first factor is liability. If it is clear that you were not at fault in the accident, then the settlement value is more than if liability is in dispute. The intensity of your collision is also a factor. "Jaws of life"-level, high-impact collisions are worth more than mere fender benders. Of course, the nature of your accident-related injuries and corresponding amount of your medical expenses are major factors.

Your past medical history will also affect your settlement value. The amount of available insurance coverage affects your settlement value by creating what is essentially a cap on the amount you can practically expect to recover. Your age, occupation, and lost wages are also a factor. Your lawyer should take all of these issues into account in crafting your settlement strategy.

Your attorney will conduct a quantum study to help determine an appropriate settlement value. This is essentially a legal research project that compares your case to other cases with similar injuries based on the amounts awarded by the trial courts and upheld by the appellate courts. Your lawyer should present you with the highest and lowest awards he or she researched and explain where your case falls within the study.

Like any compromise, a personal injury case settlement ultimately results in each party giving the other something it needs. If your case settles, it will be because the insurance company addressed your needs with a significant monetary payment. In return, it will condition payment on you signing a release of your claims against both the insurer and the driver who caused your accident. Release is the act of giving up your rights to make a claim. By agreeing to the release, you are essentially saying you will not file another lawsuit against the defendants for the same car accident and injuries. The defendants may also want to condition the settlement upon confidentiality, meaning you cannot discuss the settlement amount or negotiations with anyone.

> **FAST FACT**
> Every personal injury settlement ultimately results in each party giving the other something it needs.

Some settlements require court approval to be finalized. For example, if you are filing a case on behalf of your minor child or an incompetent person, a settlement requires court approval to be enforceable. Your attorney will have to file the settlement proposal with the court before it can be finalized.

One final issue to consider regarding your settlement is whether to demand a standard lump sum payment or a structured settlement. With a standard lump sum settlement, you would receive one check as a result of the compromise. A structured settlement is different. Under that arrangement, your settlement would be paid in installments throughout your life. Structured settlements are common when the injury is so serious that the settlement exceeds $100,000. You should consult a financial advisor to determine the respective merits of lump sum payment versus structured payout.

In closing, of course you should not settle for a lowball offer by the insurance company. It is rarely, if ever, a good idea to accept their typical initial offer of a few thousand dollars. However, a thoughtful fair market value settlement negotiated by your attorney is usually a positive outcome for you because it can save you time, money, and stress.

CHAPTER 14
The Most Important Advice

The single best way to protect your family from dangerous drivers before an accident occurs is to purchase as much uninsured/underinsured motorist bodily injury insurance coverage, also known as UM insurance, as you can afford.

To understand why UM insurance is so critically important, imagine the worst—that your spouse and children have been seriously injured in a car wreck caused by a reckless drunk driver. Your spouse has injuries to the head and spine, and needs emergency neurological surgery. It will be months, if not years, before he or she is out of bed and ready to return to work. Likewise, your kids are hurt and hospitalized indefinitely. The medical costs are astounding: over $10,000 a day for ICU treatment; more than $5,000 per day for additional hospitalizations; thousands more for X-rays, CT scans, MRI, and other diagnostic tests; tens of thousands for outpatient surgeries; and thousands more for physical therapy, rehabilitation, and prescription medications. Finally, your spouse's lost wages and additional out-of-pocket costs are staggering.

> **FAST FACT**
> The smartest way to protect yourself before an accident is to buy UM insurance.

Who will pay for these extraordinary expenses and the pain, suffering, and distress you and your family have endured through no fault of your own? The drunk driver? His or her insurance company? Your insurer?

Under Louisiana law, the person who caused the harm is liable to pay for your damages. Legally, the reckless drunk driver is responsible to your family for all damages. However, if the drunk driver is broke, he or she cannot pay you. If the drunk driver goes bankrupt, he or she will not pay you. Even the best lawyers cannot recover damages for severe injuries from a deadbeat driver who lacks money and insurance. Thus, you should never depend solely on the driver who caused the accident to cover your bills.

Of course, Louisiana law requires all drivers to carry automotive liability coverage. This is a contract between the driver and an insurance company that requires the insurer to pay damages on the driver's behalf when he or she causes a wreck that hurts someone else, like your family. However, our state only requires $15,000 of bodily injury liability insurance coverage (the lowest mandatory minimum in the country), and many drivers carry no insurance at all. So you should not count on the drunk driver's insurance for help either.

It is clearly unwise to rely on the other driver and his or her insurance company to protect your family from possible automobile accident losses. To truly protect the ones you love, you should take matters into your own hands by buying plenty of UM insurance. UM insurance is a contract between you and your car insurance company that protects your family against damages caused by uninsured motorists, underinsured motorists, and hit-and-run drivers. So if the drunk driver who injured your family had no insurance, had minimal insurance policy limits of only $15,000, or if he or she fled the scene without providing any insurance information or identification, your UM insurer must pay for your damages up to the limits of your UM policy. Therefore, you should immediately buy as much UM coverage as you can afford.

UM insurance is cheaper than liability insurance and worth every penny.

PART II:
LOUISIANA PERSONAL INJURY LAW

CHAPTER 15
Recovery of Damages

If you are injured in an auto accident, you are entitled to receive money from the person at fault in the form of damages. There are many different types of damages for which one can recover money. It is important to understand the different types and what needs to be proven to get recovery for each. When dealing with auto accidents, the term "damages" refers almost exclusively to types of monetary damages. This means that the more damages someone is awarded, the more money he or she can receive. Therefore, accident victims need to understand what types of damages they can recover for, and how much they can expect for each one.

The general idea of damages is to return the injured person, if he or she was not at fault, to the position he or she would have been in had the injury not occurred in the first place. Of course if someone has been permanently injured, disfigured, or lost a life due to an auto accident, there is no way that person can ever be returned to the same position had that accident not occurred. In situations such as these, the law requires a monetary value to be given for the person's loss.

> **FAST FACT**
> Under Louisiana law, personal injury damages are paid with money.

Sometimes the amount of damages one is able to receive for an injury can be difficult to determine. It is important to understand that an injury to a party is not limited to physical injury. In addition to physical bodily injury, "injury" can mean almost any loss that resulted from the accident, such as destruction to one's vehicle, lost wages for the time a person could not work, past and future medical expenses, and sometimes trauma caused by a person's pain and suffering. The main types of damages that can be recovered in an auto accident are:

- Property damage
- Medical expenses
- Bodily injury
- Lost wages
- Impaired earning capacity
- Pain and suffering
- Loss of enjoyment of life
- Wrongful death

The best way to determine what damages one might be entitled to is to know what is considered a loss for each of these types, and what must be proven in order to recover for them. Therefore, we need to more closely examine each of these types of damages.

PROPERTY DAMAGE

One of the most basic and easy-to-understand types of recoverable damages is damage to personal property. In the case of an automobile accident, this would primarily encompass the damage caused to one's vehicle. However, it could include damage to other personal property as well if the damage was also caused by the accident. For example, other personal belongings which were in the vehicle and damaged due to the accident, such as golf clubs or jewelry, could fall under the umbrella of damage to personal property. Not surprisingly, the amount of property damage one can expect to recover for is the total amount of property loss caused as a result of the accident. Any property that was destroyed as a result of the accident should be compensated for, but putting a value on one's property loss is more complicated.

Measure of Property Loss

Determining the actual amount awarded for property damage depends on whether or not the property was destroyed, if it is repairable, and if there was a loss of use of the property for any period of time. The normal value of recoverable property damage is the fair market value of the property if it was totally destroyed ("totaled"), or its decrease in value if it was partially destroyed. (Again, it is important to remember that when dealing with auto accidents, one's property damage is usually limited to his or her vehicle.)

> **FAST FACT**
> Your recoverable property damage is the "fair market value" of the property.

The **fair market value** for a vehicle that is totally destroyed or so badly damaged that the cost of repair exceeds 75% of its value is defined as the value of the vehicle prior to the accident minus its salvage value. The salvage value is the estimated resale value for which the destroyed vehicle can be sold as scrap. Let's say that Bob owns a truck worth $20,000, which was damaged so badly that it could not be repaired but nevertheless could be sold for a salvage value of $2,000. Bob would therefore be entitled to $18,000 in property damages. That figure represents the difference between what the truck was worth before the accident and the amount Bob will get when his truck is sold for scrap.

On the other hand, if the property can be repaired, then damages are measured by the cost to repair or restore the property. Usually this is simply determined by the actual cost of repairs that have been made or still need to be made. Alternatively, it can be calculated by figuring the difference between the value of the vehicle or other property both before and after the accident occurred. Usually, whichever figure is greater and in the injured party's best interest is the one used to determine the amount of damages. Let's say that Carol had a car worth $30,000, which was partially damaged in an accident. If the cost to repair the car was $5,000, but the value of the car was only reduced by $2,000, Carol would be granted the greater amount of $5,000 with which to repair the car.

It is important to know that when calculating the cost to repair or replace property, there are additional expenses that can be included beyond just body and mechanical repair. For example, if a piece of property is not totally destroyed, the person is entitled to damages for loss of use during the time it is being repaired. In the case of a car, the loss of use is valued at the cost of a replacement rental car for the amount of time the car is not useable. This is because property damage doesn't only include the cost of physical repair, but all other associated costs of replacement as well.

Some types of costs that can be part of a property damage award are:

- Damage to personal belongings caused by the accident
- Towing costs
- Vehicle storage fees
- Appraisals, if necessary
- Public or private property damaged by the accident
- Rental car costs
- Body shop repairs
- Replacement costs
- Diminution in resale value

As with all other types of damages, for property damages to be awarded they must be proven. This can be done through the use of repair estimates, bills, and other documentation. For this reason, it is important to keep all relevant documents related to the repairs and other costs associated to the damaged property.

PERSONAL INJURY DAMAGE

The major area of damages associated with an auto accident personal injury case are ones relating to the physical injury of a person, or multiple people, involved in the accident. There are many types of damages that can be awarded as the result of a physical injury to a person. If someone who was not at fault has been hurt in an auto accident, the injured person should seek for his or her medical expenses to be paid by the person at fault. However, there are many other effects of personal injury to consider aside from medical costs alone. Depending on the severity of the injury, a person may not be able to work or earn a living, may no longer be able to engage in pleasurable activities, or may experience undue amounts of pain and suffering. These are all problems for which damages can be awarded when a person has been injured in an auto accident.

Some of the different types of personal injury damages include:

- Past medical expenses
- Future medical expenses
- Past lost wages
- Future lost wages
- Impaired earning capacity
- Pain and suffering
- Loss of enjoyment of life

For those who have been badly injured in an auto accident, it is important to consider the full cost of their recovery and to work to obtain everything they deserve. Not all types of personal injury damages are available in every case. There are several issues that must be considered for each type of damage in order to understand when they should be sought.

Medical Expenses

If someone has been injured in an auto accident, that person can be awarded damages for medical expenses he or she has already incurred and are likely to incur in the future. It is important to consider the full scope of recovery because, depending on the type and severity of the injury, one can have long-lasting medical expenses. For example, if Stacy breaks her hip and cannot walk, it may require years of physical therapy, future surgeries, and medical attention for her to fully recover. For this reason, Stacy should seek recovery not just for her medical costs accumulated at the time of her case, but for any probable expenses that will occur even years into the future.

Some types of medical expenses an injured party can recover costs for are:

- Ambulance services
- Emergency room visits
- Physical aids and appliances
- Physical therapy
- Doctor visits
- Medical specialists
- Hospital stays
- Past and future surgeries
- Transportation costs to and from medical care
- Medication

Medical costs for serious auto accident injuries can quickly add up. The full value of these costs should be considered in determining the value of a medical expense damage award. It is also important to consider what one needs to prove in order to recover those costs.

1. Past Medical Expenses

First, we must consider what needs to be demonstrated in order to recover for medical expenses that have already been incurred by the injured person. The injured person must prove the medical treatment given, which he or she is seeking reimbursement for, was necessary based on the trauma suffered in the accident. That is to say that one can only recover damages for past medical expenses when:

- The medical expenses were due to an injury sustained in the accident, and
- The medical expenses were necessary to treat that injury.

In many cases this may be obvious, but that is not always so. For example, let's say Alex and Ben are passengers in the same car involved in a collision. If Alex breaks his leg in that collision, the emergency room cost to set and cast the leg would obviously be both necessary to treat his leg injury and incurred due to the accident. If Ben goes to the doctor a week after the collision complaining of shoulder pain, however, it may not be as obvious what the cause of his injury was. Additionally, if Ben attends two years of physical therapy for his minor shoulder discomfort, the opposing party may argue that his amount of treatment was not necessary based on his injury. Although injured parties can recover for medical expenses due to their auto accident injury, there are limits as to what can be recovered, especially without further proof.

Some things that can be used to prove that a person's medical expenses were necessary and were caused by their auto accident are:

- Medical bills
- Doctor's testimony
- Medical records
- Injured person's testimony

Medical bills are necessary and relevant to show both the cost of medical services and that the services were actually performed, but medical bills alone are not enough. They do not show whether the medical treatment given was necessary or related to the injury caused by the accident. One of the best ways to prove the validity of a claim for past medical expenses is to obtain testimony from the injured person's doctor. The person's doctor can attest to the nature and extent of his or her injuries, the treatment given, and the need for such treatment.

A doctor's testimony, however, should not be the only thing relied upon to prove medical expenses. Medical and hospital records should be used, and are important for proof because they document the diagnosis and treatment of the patient. They often can be used to verify that the medical services, supplies, and medication for which the injured person is seeking compensation were, in fact, given, as well as the reasons why they were given.

Proving that the medical expenses were actually incurred is rarely the biggest issue, though. Instead, proving that the costs were reasonable, the services were needed, and the injury was caused by the accident can be more important. Some of the arguments defendants will often use are that the injured party continued to take treatment after the symptoms and conditions were resolved, that the injured party did not seek prompt treatment, that the injury was a pre-existing condition, or that the injury was not caused by the accident.

As touched on in the example above with Ben, a person who

has inflated medical expenses because he or she continues to seek treatment long after the injury is healed will have a harder time recovering then a person who has a genuine need.

In the previous example, if Ben sought to recover the cost of two years' worth of physical therapy for his minor shoulder discomfort, he could be accused of malingering with his treatment, and he risks not recovering the full cost of his therapy. However, if there was a genuine need, there are many ways to prove the treatment was necessary.

It is also extremely important to seek prompt treatment. A person is not allowed to recover medical costs that could have been avoided by a reasonable effort of the injured person. The practical outcome is that if an injury is aggravated or made much worse because the injured person refused to seek medical attention, then the injured person puts him- or herself at risk of not recovering the full cost of medical treatment. For example, let's say that instead of waiting one week to see a doctor about his shoulder, Ben waited three months. In that time, his minor injury turned into a major one because he continued to lift heavy boxes at work, since he did not consult a doctor to tell him otherwise. If he now needs major surgery for the injury, he may not be able to recover all of his medical costs, because his delay contributed significantly to the severity of the injury. Although some symptoms may not appear for weeks or even months after an accident, it is important to seek prompt treatment at the time one becomes aware of an injury, not later.

> **FAST FACT**
> Seek prompt medical attention after your accident for a full financial recovery.

As a general rule, costs associated with an injury that existed prior to the time of the auto accident are not recoverable. There are certain situations in which this is not entirely true, however. Defendants will often argue that medical costs should not be paid if the injured party suffered past injuries that were of a similar nature. This is based on the argument that the injury could have been a **pre-existing condition**. A pre-existing injury would not be the result of the accident, and therefore is not recoverable. Let's say Ben had suffered a shoulder injury in the past, and since his auto accident has complained of shoulder pain. Defendants will argue that his shoulder injury already existed at the time of the accident and therefore was not caused by it. A defendant will further argue that the current medical expenses were only necessary because of the previous injury, and that there would not have been a need for medical treatment if it were not for the pre-existing shoulder injury.

This argument can be countered by showing that the person had fully recovered from the injury prior to the accident, or by showing that the earlier injury was aggravated or worsened as a result of the accident. In short, even if there were a pre-existing injury, if the injury was made worse as a direct result of the accident, then the injured person can recover the medical costs associated with that aggravation. If Ben's shoulder injury was fully recovered prior to the accident, or was not fully recovered but was worsened because of it, the at-fault party is responsible for his medical costs. This is true even if a healthy person in the same situation would not have been injured. Even though Ben's shoulder is more sensitive to injury because it had not fully healed, this is not an excuse for the defendants to avoid payment. Although a previous injury is not the direct responsibility of the person at fault, the defendants must take the injured party or parties "as they find

> **FAST FACT**
> Pre-existing injuries that are not the result of the accident are not recoverable, but if the accident aggravated an injury, the worsening of that injury is compensable.

them." This means that they are responsible for any further injuries caused to that specific person—in this case, Ben.

2. Future Medical Expenses
Sometimes if an injury is very severe, an injured person can be entitled to costs related to future medical expenses. Some injuries can have lifelong medical costs associated with them. A person is entitled to costs for future medical expenses if it is reasonably certain that future medical expenses will be required. The need for future medical coverage can be difficult to prove, and much harder to value. The need can result from the original injury or from an increased susceptibility to future injuries. Since these costs are highly speculative, it sometimes can be difficult to show that the need is highly likely, but it can be proven with supporting medical testimony and estimations of the likely cost of these expenses.

Imagine James is hit by a tractor-trailer and temporarily disabled, such that it will take years of therapy and possibly future surgeries for him to walk again. In a situation such as this one, it should not be difficult to show the need for future medical expenses. Every injury is different, however, and it can be difficult to determine the need, especially when dealing with less severe injuries. Although this need may not be as obvious for all injuries, it is important to know that this type of relief is available.

Lost Wages and Impaired Earning Capacity

There are several broader impacts of being injured in an accident beyond medical costs alone. One of those is a person's possible inability to earn a living. If an injury has prevented someone from working for living, then the injured person is entitled to recover damages for time lost from his or her job. The amount of money that can be recovered for being out of work depends on how much the injured person is paid, how long a period he or she was unable to work, whether he or she is ever able to work again, or if he or she will not be able to work in the same capacity as before the accident. A person's inability to earn a wage, or to earn the same wages as prior to his or her injury, is usually classified as one of three types of damages: past lost wages, future lost wages, and impaired earning capacity.

1. Past Lost Wages
An injured person who was employed at the time of an accident is entitled to recover damages for wages, commissions, bonuses, tips, etc., that he or she is unable to collect because of absence from the job due to injury. For example, if Greg has missed three months of work at his construction job due to his auto accident back injury, he may be able to recover those lost wages. The amount of past lost wages does not need to be proven to a mathematical certainty, but must be well established by the evidence.

To establish the amount of lost wages to which Greg is entitled, several items can be used, which include:

- Testimony of an employer
- Payroll records
- W-2s
- Tax returns
- Pay stubs
- Social Security records

In addition, the amount of time the injured person is out of work must not be excessive for the injury, and must be shown to be medically necessary. This means that the length of time Greg has missed work due to his back injury must be proportionate to the severity of that injury.

For people who are self-employed, the amount of lost wages

can be more difficult to determine, depending on their type of self-employment. In these cases, damage awards for lost wages may be made proportionately to the lost profits or reduced earning capacity of their business. Since a business might still be able to generate income for the injured party even though he or she is not able to work, the amount of recovery for lost profits will be heavily dependent on the injured party's personal effort required to generate profits for his or her business. For example, if a self-employed doctor is injured and unable to see patients, his practice will likely not be able to generate much income without his personal efforts. On the other hand, a restaurant owner who merely oversees the operation of his restaurant may not suffer as much in the way of lost profits, and therefore will have a smaller claim for recovery.

> **FAST FACT**
> If you miss work due to accident related injuries, you are entitled to recover damages for lost wages.

It is important to note that with past lost wages, as well the other types of damages for lost or reduced wages, even an unemployed person can still recover in limited circumstances. A person who regularly works, but is unemployed at the time of the accident, is entitled to damages for wages he or she could have otherwise earned. However, that person still has a burden of proving what his or her earnings would have been and that he or she would have likely been employed in the near future if not for the injury sustained.

2. Future Lost Wages

When a person has been injured so severely that he or she will never be able to return to work or will not return for a long time, those individuals can recover compensation for their future lost wages. Damage awards for future lost wages are more difficult to prove because they are inherently speculative. One must do more than show a difference between the injured person's income before and after the accident. It must be shown instead that the person's **earning capacity** has been reduced. This means the award is not based on whether the person has been working since his or her accident, but whether he or she has the ability to work moving forward.

For example, it is not enough to show that Greg has not been working since his injury. To make a valid claim, one must medically demonstrate why Greg will not be able to work in the future. Greg's inability to work, however, does not need to constitute a permanent inability to work or the inability to work any job. If Greg will likely be out of work for an additional six months, he can make a claim for six months' worth of future lost wages. Also, perhaps Greg is a skilled carpenter, but due to his injury he cannot work as such. He is instead limited to working as a checkout clerk and earns much less money. He can make a claim of future lost wages for the difference in income he can no longer receive until he is able to return to work as a carpenter. To recover for future lost wages, injured parties must show that they are no longer physically able to work for a period time, or that due to the injury sustained they must take an alternate type of employment that does not allow them to match their previous income.

> **FAST FACT**
> Lost earning capacity claims focus on whether you have the ability to work moving forward.

Some factors that determine the amount of damages for future lost wages include:

- Age of the injured person
- Life expectancy
- Work life expectancy

- Investment income factor
- Productivity increase
- Prospects for rehabilitation
- Future earning capacity
- Loss of future earning capacity
- Loss of earning ability
- Inflation

To prove the need for lost future wages, it is important to medically show 1) the amount of time required for recovery, 2) if full recovery is ever likely, and 3) the length of the medical treatment that is keeping the person from working at his or her job. This is important because if the injured party is not permanently disabled, the amount of time the person is unable to work is often a point of contention among the parties. If the injured party is able to take alternative employment, future lost wages are available if that type of employment does not pay the same amount.

If the injured person is unemployed at the time of the accident, it does not completely bar him or her from recovering future lost wages. If those parties seek to recover, though, they have a high burden of proving they had the intent to find employment. Previous work history can be used to prove the intent of the unemployed individual to find work. If the injured person has no work history and no explanation for his or her unemployment, that person is not likely to recover for future lost wages.

While not obtainable for all types of injuries, it is important to know this type of recovery is available for more seriously injured persons who cannot return to work for a longer period of time.

3. Impaired Earning Capacity
The damage award for impaired earning capacity is similar to that of future lost wages. It is available when an injured person is not

able to earn the same income that he or she could prior to being injured. Impaired earning capacity is a broader way of compensating for lost future wages, and includes one's inability to advance to an alternative career or better-paying position. Even if an injured person is able to return to his or her previous employment and earn the same amount of money as before the accident, that person can be awarded damages for impaired earning capacity if he or she is unable to advance in his or her career due to the injury sustained. For this reason, an injured person's actual income is not the determining factor for impaired earning capacity.

For example, let's say Allen is an engineering student who was working part-time as a landscaper to pay for school. If Allen suffered a head injury in an auto accident that prohibited him from ever becoming an engineer, his future salary as an engineer could no longer be earned. This means his future earning capacity would be greatly impaired. In this way, the value of one's impaired earning capacity can be difficult to predict. Unlike past lost wages, it is based on the earning capacity of the individual before and after the accident occurred. To establish this, one would have to consider how much the injured person's condition disadvantages them in the work force.

Impaired earning capacity can also include a person's chance of promotion or transfer to a higher-paying job. If a person missed out on a promotion because of absence from work, then a claim for impaired earning capacity can be made. Another situation which might be considered is if he or she is unable to move to a higher-paying job because of a physical disability caused by his or her injury. It is important to note that this sort of impairment must be related to a specific situation, and not mere speculation of a better-paying position. It must be shown that a specific position was available and, if not for the injury, the injured person would very likely have been able to achieve the position based on his or her capabilities and qualifications. Mere speculation that one will not be able to obtain a promotion or better job in the future because of an injury is not sufficient.

As with promotions, the injured party must prove the inability to achieve future career goals by showing that they were specifically being pursued. In the case of Allen, the engineering student, it would be easy to prove that he was pursuing a different career. However, if he had not yet entered school and was still able to work as a landscaper, it would be much more difficult for him to recover for impaired earning capacity.

Pain and Suffering

Another type of damages for which an injured party can seek compensation is the pain and suffering the person will endure as a result of his or her injury. This is generally the component of the personal injury claim that has the greatest value. The amount of damages that can be obtained depends on the severity and duration of the injured person's pain and suffering. There are several types of ailments from which someone can suffer, besides physical pain, that can be a considered a component of pain and suffering.

Some conditions included in pain and suffering (aside from physical discomfort and trauma) are:

- Fright
- Nervousness
- Grief
- Anxiety
- Shock
- Humiliation
- Apprehension
- Mental anguish

To recover for pain and suffering, the condition must have resulted from a physical impact. This means that although the injury does not have to be major, pain and suffering must be the result of a bodily (and not an emotional) injury. If one was only a witness to an accident, then there is no recovery for any perceived pain and suffering for witnessing the accident, except under extreme situations which will not likely apply with automobile accidents.

In order to recover for this type of damages, the different aspects of the person's pain and suffering—such as the location, frequency, nature, and type of suffering—must be specifically demonstrated. Since "pain and suffering" is a highly subjective term, it must be shown in as much detail as possible; otherwise an injured party risks being perceived as exaggerating or making up their suffering. The injured party should be able to describe the nature (sharp, dull, aching, cramping, etc.), length (constant, intermittent), aggravating conditions (weather, particular movements, fatigue), and any objective symptoms (headaches, nausea, insomnia, limping) of the pain and suffering. Since legal cases often move slowly, it is a good idea to keep a diary of the pain and suffering endured in case the person later recovers and does not remember the details of his or her injury. It is also a good idea, whenever possible, to take photos or videos of injuries and the pain and suffering associated with those injuries. Since the person could later recover from the injury, it is good to have as much photographic evidence of the injury and related pain as possible.

> **FAST FACT**
> Keep a journal and/or take photos and video of your car accident injury pain and suffering to help prove your case for damages.

A patient's medical records, testimony from his or her doctor, and even testimony from friends, family, and other eyewitnesses can be used to try and prove a person's pain and suffering. Since these types of claims are hard to document, defendants will always try to argue against them. If an injured person was observed engaging in activities inconsistent with the injury sustained, then it would significantly hurt his or her case. For example, if a person is found to have been lifting heavy boxes after claiming he suffered severe pain from a back injury, that person would hurt his chances of recovering for pain and suffering. The same is the case for a person who claims to be humiliated about a bad facial scar she suffered, but was heard telling her friends that it didn't bother her very much. As with the other more speculative damages, the need for this must be real and severe in order for it to be obtained—but it is important to know that it is available to those who are greatly suffering from their injuries.

As with past medical expenses, if the injured person's pain and suffering could have been avoided or reduced, but he or she did not seek prompt medical attention, then that person's damages for pain and suffering will likely be reduced accordingly. This means that if the person's condition worsened because he or she avoided seeing a doctor for several months and the delay was the cause of the pain and suffering, then that person likely cannot recover. For that reason it is important to seek prompt medical attention and to well document one's case for pain and suffering.

Loss of Enjoyment of Life

When a person has been injured, it may prevent him or her from participating in some of the same activities as he or she previously did. Damages for loss of enjoyment of life are similar to pain and suffering, but instead they are awarded for a person's inability to engage in pleasurable activities as a result of the injury sustained. The distinction between the two is that with loss of enjoyment of life, something specific is taken away from the victim, as opposed to the general suffering from physical pain or mental anguish.

For example, if Stacy is a college student and was severely injured to the point where she was disabled, had to drop out of school, and moved home with her parents, this could constitute a loss of enjoyment of life. Stacy would no longer be able to continue with her college life activities and would become greatly reliant on her parents. Therefore, in addition to the pain and suffering Stacy may endure, she also has a strong claim for loss of enjoyment of life, because she is unable to live her life as she could before.

> **FAST FACT**
> Loss of enjoyment of life damages are awarded for a person's inability to engage in pleasurable activities as a result of his or her injury.

In order to recover for this type of damages, the injured person would have to show that the injury was more than a mere inconvenience. As such, the condition would likely need to be permanent and irreversible, and the loss would have to be to an important part of his or her life. If Jack was only an occasional weekend golfer and could no longer golf due to injury, this is not likely to be considered a loss of enjoyment of life. If, on the other hand, Jack was an avid amateur golfer, played frequently, took great pride in his golf achievements, and could show that golf was a big part of his life, then permanently and irreversibly losing the ability to play golf may be something for which he is able to recover damages. Although the circumstances for this are not met in every auto accident, it is important to know that this type of relief is available to those who can no longer participate in important activities.

CONSORTIUM CLAIMS

When you make the important decision to file a personal injury lawsuit after your automobile accident, it is critical that you and your attorney list all the ways in which you and your family have been harmed. Your lawsuit is the only chance you will get to be compensated for that particular accident. Think about it as though you are making your weekly grocery list. You must list all of the ingredients you need to make all of your meals for the week, and then you make one trip to the store. You do not have time to go the grocery store multiple times, so if you forget something, you must do without it. A consortium claim must be included in the list of damages your attorney requests from the court, or this claim is lost forever. A consortium claim does not speak to the way you personally have been harmed in the accident. Instead, this claim is about how your automobile accident affected your spouse and family.

A loss of consortium claim is another way of stating that your accident and your injuries negatively impacted your family. A loss of consortium claim allows your family members to be awarded money for the harm and extra burden your accident caused them. Your accident and the injuries you sustained may have caused you to miss spending quality time with your family, or you might have been unable to provide financially for a period of time, or perhaps you were unable to do simple household chores like cut the grass. All of these harms and burdens that your accident caused your family to experience are compensable in the same way that you can be awarded money for your personal pain and suffering.

The following people can bring a loss of consortium claim for damages they sustained from your automobile accident:

- Your spouse
- Your child or children
- Your mother and father
- Your brothers and sisters
- Your grandfather and grandmother

Only the people on this list are allowed to bring a loss of consortium claim under Louisiana law. (This list does include adoptive relationships.)

Much of your focus after your automobile accident was probably on treating your physical injuries and repairing the damage to your vehicle. The first priority of a personal injury suit for an automobile accident is getting you compensated for these harms and burdens. However, as discussed above, it is very likely that your family was also negatively impacted by your car accident. There are many adjustments your family probably had to make after your car accident. These burdens are compensated through a loss of consortium claim.

> **FAST FACT**
> Loss of consortium claims allow your family members to be awarded money for the harm and extra burden your accident caused them.

A loss of consortium claim can be brought if your family experiences one or more of the following elements:

- Loss of love and affection
- Loss of society and companionship
- Impairment of sexual relations
- Loss of performance of material services
- Loss of financial support
- Loss of aid and assistance
- Loss of fidelity

It is not enough that your family member was mentally upset or distressed about your automobile accident. While this is an understandable and expected reaction, there has to be something more for the court to award your family damages for their loss of consortium claim. A loss of consortium claim will be successful if your family members can point to specific instances where they experienced one or more of the elements listed above. For example, if you missed several of a child's sporting events, this is compensable in a loss of consortium claim for loss of society and companionship. If your spouse was forced to do all of the household chores for a period, this is also compensable in a loss of consortium claim for loss of performance of material services. It is best to list as many specific facts where your life was negatively altered as a result of the car accident so that your attorney can fit these instances in the list of compensable elements above.

There are some important limits to note. First, you cannot "marry into" a loss of consortium claim. What this means is that if you are engaged and your fiancé gets into a car accident, you cannot file a loss of consortium claim after you get married. Your loss of consortium award amount is also limited by insurance policies. The accident victim and the person claiming loss of consortium are generally treated together, as if they are one person, for the purpose of insurance policies and "per person" limits on damages. The final limit to remember on loss of consortium awards is that compensation is ultimately up to the judge or jury and how they are feeling on that particular day.

Loss of consortium damages are discretionary, meaning that judges or juries can award a staggeringly large amount or none at all. Generally, judges and juries are not big fans of loss of consortium awards, and in many cases loss of consortium awards are denied because after the accident the victim was able to spend more time with the family member who is claiming loss of consortium. It is still wise to list all of the ways your family has been impacted by your auto accident so that your attorney can advise you on whether to file a loss of consortium claim.

PUNITIVE DAMAGES

Punitive damages are the only type of damages granted that are not based on any actual injury or damage to the injured person. Although punitive damages are rare, it is still important to understand what they are. Punitive damages are given in addition to other damages to punish the person at fault or to deter others from engaging in similar actions. They are not granted based on damage or harm sustained by the injured person, but based on the seriousness of the action of the at-fault driver. It is important to note that in Louisiana, punitive damages are generally NOT allowed in personal injury cases.

However, punitive damages are important to mention because one of the few exceptions in which punitive damages can be awarded is in the case of drinking and driving. They can be allowed when the person causing the accident had been driving while intoxicated. Courts allow punitive damages in this case because the act of drinking and driving shows a reckless disregard for the safety of others. If the intoxication was the cause of the accident, then courts will sometimes add punitive damages in addition to the other damages, in order to more severely punish that person for driving while intoxicated. They are even allowed to award these damages when there has only been injury to property.

> **FAST FACT**
> Drunk driving accidents are a rare exception to the rule that punitive damages are not available in Louisiana car accident personal injury cases.

Although punitive damages are rarely awarded in Louisiana, if an intoxicated driver was the cause of the auto accident, there is a possibility that punitive damages can be given.

CHAPTER 16
What You Must Prove to Win Your Case

At the most basic level, all you need to prove to win your auto accident personal injury case is that you suffered injuries that were caused by someone else's mistakes. Of course, it is rarely that simple once a giant insurance company and its high-powered lawyers get involved. To make matters worse, many potential jurors possess tainted views about personal injury lawyers and the victims they represent. Think about it—chances are that before you or your family member were injured, you held personal injury attorneys and their clients in low regard. Unfortunately, that belief is all too common in Louisiana. The myth that all injury plaintiffs are greedy fakers has been exaggerated far beyond the unfortunate reality that a small minority of claims are fraudulent. The consequence is an uphill climb toward proving your case.

When you are a victim involved in an automobile accident, you understandably will want the party that is at fault, and/or his or her insurance company, to pay for your injuries and other damages from the accident. Often, it is easy to determine which party or parties are at fault for an accident—but not always. No matter the difficulty, you must also think about what kind of proof you will need to win a lawsuit or have a favorable settlement against that party. This chapter outlines the kinds of proof you will need to win your personal injury case.

Generally speaking, car accidents in Louisiana will be governed by tort laws using the *negligence* standard. Whenever you are suing for negligence, the assignment of fault plays a major role in how your case will turn out. Louisiana is a pure *comparative fault* state.

What this means is that the fault is broken down by party, and a percentage is assigned to each party as to how much each is at fault for the accident—including you. Therefore, whenever some of the fault is assigned to you, your portion of fault will lower the amount of damages that you can receive from the party or parties whom you are suing. Because of this, it is important—as always—for you to be a safe driver, because any mistakes or bad judgment in an accident can be assigned to you as your percentage of fault. Once you prove the parts of a negligence case, the allocation of fault in the accident will be decided.

PROVING THE ELEMENTS OF NEGLIGENCE

In a negligence case in Louisiana, you must prove the following five items to have a strong case:

1. The party at fault had a *duty* to behave a certain way;
2. The party at fault *breached* the duty;
3. The breach was the *cause in fact* of the injuries or damages;
4. The damages were in the *scope of the breach*; and
5. *Actual damages* and injuries were caused to you.

Some of these elements are more difficult to prove or explain than others. However, you must successfully prove them all in order to win your case and recover for your injuries and damages.

The ability to prove that the other party is totally at fault for the accident, or has as much percentage of fault as possible, is crucial to your case once you establish the six elements of negligence. To do this, you and your representatives will sometimes have to go through great lengths to find—and preserve—evidence and testimony. Throughout this chapter, I will suggest some steps that you should take after an accident in order to find such evidence. However, it is important to remember that before you begin, you should receive any medical care necessary to ensure any injuries you have do not worsen. In other words, if you

> **FAST FACT**
> Proving all five elements of negligence gives you the best chance of recovering damages from the at-fault party.

are seriously injured in an accident, the first priority should be getting medical attention, not finding evidence or proving the elements of negligence.

The *rule of law* is a legal term that describes what the party at fault should have done in the situation, as opposed to the course of action that party took. In order to prove this part of the negligence case, you and your lawyer must come up with the correct action to take in the situation. For example, if you were driving down a three-lane highway and a car swerved into your lane to avoid something in the road while the lane on the other side of the driver was clear, you could argue the that correct action was to swerve the opposite way and not into your car.

In reality, cases may not be as clear cut as this. Identifying a rule of law may be more difficult if there were not many other options for the at-fault driver other than to hit your car while swerving. Your lawyer will likely have insight on this matter and be able to identify a rule of law for your situation. It can help your case if the rule of law is obvious in the situation and is in stark contrast to the action that the party at fault took. For example, the requirement to stop at a red light would be such a rule of law. Establishing that there was a better choice of action is an important starting point to winning your negligence case against the party at fault in your automobile accident.

Proving a Duty

If you have been involved in an automobile accident, proving that the driver at fault had *a duty* could potentially be the easiest or hardest part of your case. Basically, you have to prove that the party at fault had a legal duty to act—or not act—a certain way in the situation. The court will sometimes use the "reasonable person" standard to calibrate the duty owed by the party at fault. This standard takes into account different actions and circumstances surrounding an accident, and determines how a reasonable person would act under the same or similar circumstances. Therefore, the analysis of what duty is owed to you is somewhat subjective.

Here are a few of the many duties that all motorists in Louisiana must comply with at all times:

- Operate, control, and use their vehicle reasonably, and maintain a proper lookout for hazards which might pose an unreasonable risk of harm.
- See that which should be seen and observe all traffic signs.
- Drive defensively from the time the driver witnesses a negligent operation of another vehicle, or notices other hazards.
- Keep attention focused on the roadway and not get distracted by the many things that could distract a person. (That duty is owed to others in the driver's vehicle, as well as those in other vehicles on the roadway.)
- Exercise a greater degree of care in adverse conditions, such as bad weather or darkness.

At trial, it is necessary for you and your lawyer to explain to the court how a reasonable person would act in the situation. For example, a driver has a duty to drive in his or her lane and to avoid switching lanes unless it is safe and clear to do so. Assuming that there are no extenuating circumstances, the duty the driver has to others is to wait to switch lanes until the neighboring lane is clear. If an individual is driving in his or her lane and sideswipes you by immediately switching lanes for no apparent reason, that person violated his or her duty to you. However, the situation would be different if there were an obstruction in the road that caused the party at fault to switch lanes abruptly. The court may believe that an abrupt lane change may be what a reasonable person may have done in that situation, depending on the size and danger of the obstruction. Proving a duty can be a bit more nuanced than it first seems.

As seen from the above example, proving that another person had a duty to you can be quite easy, but can also be difficult when certain circumstances come into play. Generally speaking, though, drivers have duties to one another. If these duties did not exist, the roads would be even more dangerous than they are now. The important takeaway from this section is that you must establish that the driver who hit you had a duty to not do so. If you prove this, your next step is proving that he or she breached that duty.

Proving Breach of the Duty

As discussed above, proving that the party you are suing had a duty is an essential element of your negligence case. Next, you must prove that a breach of duty occurred. This can also vary in difficulty. Just like above, whenever you seek to prove a breach of duty has occurred, the standard used to determine whether there was a breach is the "reasonable person" standard. This standard measures the way that the party at fault acted as compared to the way a reasonable person would act in the situation. If the actions of the party at fault are different than the actions of a "reasonable person," by definition there was a breach of duty. The deviation between the actions of the party at fault and the reasonable person will determine the severity of the breach.

You may be asking, "What does this all mean?" It can be a confusing analysis, because most of these cases hinge largely on situation-specific issues. This can make it hard to determine what exactly a "reasonable person" would do in a particular situation, and whether the party at fault actually breached. Whether you can prove a breach often boils down to what evidence you have. If you know what the breach is but cannot prove it, your case is not as strong.

The following are some important practices for collecting evidence that you should undertake after your accident, if possible. Some of these should be done at the time of the accident, but others can wait.

1. Identify Witnesses
Identifying witnesses who saw your automobile accident can be crucial to the success of your case. They can corroborate your story, as well as provide insight about your accident that you may not have even realized. While passengers in your vehicle can be excellent witnesses, independent third-party witnesses are even better because their credibility is more difficult to challenge. The importance of witnesses cannot be understated. It is critical that you make sure to get their contact information, as well as have them provide statements to law enforcement officers (or, at the very least, to you). This way, you can use their accounts as evidence that can prove that the party at fault did, in fact, breach his or her duty when the accident occurred. If you are physically able, do everything you can to locate witnesses. The ability to prove a breach may depend solely on this factor.

2. Take Photos of the Accident
Taking photographs of the scene of the accident may also provide essential evidence. Elements such as the placement of the cars can potentially prove that a breach happened. However, if

you are trying to prove that someone other than a driver was at fault (such as a homeowner who left a branch hanging too low in a tree), a photo taken reasonably soon after the accident can be equally important. As with identifying witnesses, getting photographs of the scene can be time sensitive. Therefore, consider the time-sensitivity of the kind of breach you are trying to prove when planning your efforts to take pictures.

Proving the Cause in Fact

In Louisiana, before reaching the question of duty and breach in a negligence case, the court determines whether the party at fault's actions were the *cause in fact* of the injuries and damages. To do this, the court considers how directly the injuries were related to the actions of the person you are suing. The closer they are tied together, the stronger your case will be. You will want to prove that the act of the party at fault and your injuries are very intertwined in order to strengthen your case.

There are many different kinds of cause, but I will focus on four here:

1. Sole cause
2. But-for cause
3. Substantial factor
4. Motivating factor

Generally, a **sole cause** of an accident may be proven where the party at fault is clearly the only cause of the accident. If you can prove this, you will have the strongest case.

The second test, **but-for causation**, is more common in the courts. This kind of causation is the theory that but for the act of the other party, the injury would not have occurred. For example, assume you are hit by someone who runs a red light. "But for" the party at fault running the red light, the accident would not have happened. The but-for case is close to the sole cause case, and the closer you can connect the injury to the act, the better your case will be. However, some cases have more than one but-for cause. An example of such a situation would be a multi-car accident wherein multiple vehicles share the fault for the collision.

The substantial factor and motivating factor are similar and potentially help your case, but likely less than the above two causes. If the breach played a large role in your accident but maybe was not the *but-for* cause, it was likely a **substantial factor** in the accident. For example, consider a multi-car accident in which a car running a red light might force another vehicle to divert into your lane and hit you. In that case, the court may find that the first car is a substantial factor in your accident by causing the second car to swerve, and the second car's action the but-for cause in your damages. Finally, if the breach had something to do with the harm, but the harm was somewhat disconnected or far from the breach, it is likely a **motivating factor**, which is the least convincing.

The overall aim is to show that the action of your opposing party caused your damages and injuries. The closer you tie the actions of the at-fault driver to the accident in which you received damages, the better your case will be. You may have little control over this factor, but the "cause in fact" element is essential for proving a negligence case.

Proving Scope of the Duty and Breach

Once you have proved that there was a duty and a breach of said duty, you have to prove that the injury that happened to you was meant to be prevented by the rule of law or duty (the duty-damages connection). In other words, you have to show some kind of association between the rule of law and the harm that was caused to you. In an automobile accident, you will obviously argue that the rule of law is intended to protect other drivers as well as pedestrians. You must further explain that the action the party at fault should have taken would have prevented your injury—and was intended to do so.

For example, if the rule of law is that a driver should check his or her blind spot before switching lanes, the harm to be prevented is harm to drivers in the adjacent lanes. If a driver changed lanes without checking his or her blind spot and then hit you, the harm you receive from this accident would be within the scope of the duty and rule of law.

When you are involved in an accident, connecting your damages to the breach of duty owed is a crucial element to prove in a negligence analysis. Also, just like proving many of these elements, this can be easy or difficult at times. It simply depends on the facts surrounding your automobile accident. Linking your injuries and damages to the rule of law and/or duty of the party at fault is necessary to win your case.

Proving Damages

Proving damages is the last—but not least important—element of proving your negligence case. If you cannot prove that any damages resulted from the accident, you cannot win a negligence case. You should document all damages and injuries received from the accident. However, most of the time you will obviously be able to prove at least some damages in an automobile accident. For instance, your vehicle will show evidence of damage from where you were hit. In general, this is not a terribly difficult part of the negligence analysis to prove, but it is necessary to winning your case.

TYING IT ALL TOGETHER

In order to win your personal injury case, particularly if it involves negligence by another driver, you must prove all of the above elements. If you are successful, fault will be allocated to all responsible parties to determine the amount of your recovery. Each step is crucial and, again, will vary in difficulty based on the situational factors of your case. Consulting with an experienced personal injury attorney will help in understanding your rights.

CHAPTER 17
Presumptions of Fault

When you are involved in an automobile accident, you may wonder how the court or jury will determine who is at fault in the accident. In most negligence cases, you must prove all of the steps of a negligence case, which were outlined in the previous chapter. However, there are certain situations where there is a presumption of fault for one of the drivers. A presumption of fault is essentially what its name suggests. Whenever there is a presumption of fault against a party, it means that the party is assumed to be at fault in the accident. In effect, the party who was hit in the accident will not have to initially prove negligence of the party who hit them, because the other party is already presumed to be at fault for the accident. The party against whom the presumption is asserted must rebut this assertion in order to win in court. Basically, this means that the presumed at-fault party must prove to the court or jury that he or she was not negligent.

Certain presumptions of fault in Louisiana are common to automobile accidents, and these are particularly relevant when the court is allocating fault to determine what damages will be provided. If you are a victim in an automobile accident and there is a presumption of fault against the individual who hit you, you

> **FAST FACT**
> In certain types of car accidents, Louisiana law will automatically presume that one party is at fault unless that party is able to prove otherwise.

can potentially maximize your monetary award in the case. It is important to remember that the person against whom the presumption of fault applies can rebut this presumption, though. Once they do this, fault can be allocated to you in the case.

IMPORTANT PRESUMPTIONS OF FAULT IN LOUISIANA

On a state-by-state basis, presumptions of fault can vary. In Louisiana, there are a couple of presumptions that are particularly important to automobile accidents. The two most relevant of these have to do with 1) rear-end collisions, and 2) left-turning motorists.

Presumption of Fault for Rear-End Collisions

A rear-end collision is an accident in which one car hits the back of another car. They are common, and they can cause many damages to both the vehicle and the driver. In this kind of car accident, there is a presumption that the driver who hit the other driver from behind is at fault for the accident. This presumption is relatively well known, and the reasoning behind it is sound. The courts have reasoned that this presumption should exist because usually the driver of a car that hits another car from behind is either not paying attention or acting negligently in some other way. Additionally, Louisiana laws state that drivers should not follow the vehicle ahead of them in a way that is unreasonable or imprudent. In other words, drivers should not drive too closely to the car in front of them.

Generally, it is assumed that the driver who was rear-ended did not cause the accident. Therefore, if you are rear-ended in an automobile accident and you were not acting negligently, there is a good chance that the presumption of fault will help you recover damages from the person who hit you. However, as discussed above, the party against whom the presumption of fault applies can rebut this presumption in order to place some of the fault on you. Therefore, this could lower the amount of money they would have to pay you if you won the case.

There are two ways in Louisiana that this presumption can be rebutted. The first is that the driver has to show 1) that the driver had control of the vehicle, 2) that the driver observed the vehicle in front of him or her closely, and 3) that he or she kept a safe and reasonable distance from the vehicle. Alternatively, he or she can prove that the driver whom he or she hit was driving negligently and caused a hazard that he or she simply could not avoid. While the presumption of fault is rebuttable, it is a difficult presumption to overcome. Therefore, if you are rear-ended in an accident, this presumption will likely help you win your case.

Presumption of Fault for Left-Turning Drivers

When an automobile accident involves someone who is turning left, a presumption of fault is held against the driver who is turning. The left turn is generally considered a dangerous maneuver, and if it is established that an accident occurred while a driver was attempting to turn left, then the driver who was turning is at fault. This presumption exists because someone who is turning left is intentionally entering the lane of another driver to complete a driving maneuver. Whenever a driver is attempting to turn left, he or she has an obligation to signal, as well as to judge the traffic in front of and behind him or her in order to ensure that the turn can be completed safely at that time. If you are hit by a driver who is turning left, your ability to win your case against that individual is strong.

As with drivers who rear-end other drivers, the driver who is turning left can rebut this presumption. In order to do this, he or she would have to prove that the driver whom he or she hit was acting negligently in some way. Some possibilities are that the other driver was driving too fast, or that the other driver had time to stop and should have been aware of the left-turning driver in the intersection, but did not take action to mitigate the damages. Additionally, left-turning drivers can obviously escape this presumption whenever they have a green turning signal at an intersection and they are struck by a car traveling in the opposite direction.

Generally, though, this presumption is difficult for the left-turning driver to overcome. Therefore, if you are struck by a driver who is turning left, you have a very strong chance of winning your case on this presumption alone.

HOW A PRESUMPTION OF FAULT STRENGTHENS YOUR CASE

If you are injured in an automobile accident involving a rear-end collision or a left-turning driver, it definitely behooves you to pursue a personal injury claim if you were driving responsibly. These kinds of accidents will provide you with a case that is easier to win than most, and you will likely be able to recover damages in such a case. When you are involved in one of these kinds of accidents, you should make sure that there are witnesses to corroborate what happened and/or police reports documenting what happened on the scene. If you can establish a rear-end collision or that a left-turning driver caused a collision in court, your odds of winning your case will dramatically increase.

CHAPTER 18
Beware of Social Media

Think before you click! Louisiana law allows the information you share on social networking sites like Facebook to be legally used against you. One foolish post, pin, photo, or tweet could doom your personal injury case.

Facebook and other social networks are public forums—even if your profile is set to private. Facebook now has over a billion active users, and an increasing number of them are facing legal problems as a result of the info they share with their online "friends." This could hurt your career, your family life, and your personal injury claim.

The number of people fired or not hired due to Facebook is on the rise. Almost half of all employers use social networks to screen job candidates. Moreover, Louisiana is an *employment-at-will* state, meaning that your employer may usually fire, suspend, or discipline you for any reason except a few illegal grounds (race, gender, whistle-blowing, etc.). So, if you complain about your boss on Facebook, or if you post a picture of yourself tailgating at the LSU game after calling in sick, he or she may fire you.

> **FAST FACT**
> Louisiana law allows social media sharing to be used against you in court.

Use of Facebook information in court cases is increasing due to lawyers mining online profiles for evidence. You may have postings that could hurt your case, even if they were shared by someone other than you. The most common area of Facebook evidence is family law, namely divorce and child custody proceedings. Imagine a defendant who claims to be a loyal husband and great father, yet his future ex-wife's lawyer found barroom photos on Facebook that show him carousing with women when he claimed he was watching the kids! Such pictures may be admissible at trial.

Facebook photos or posts can likewise doom a personal injury case. Consider the auto accident plaintiff who claims a back injury prevents him from working or enjoying physical activities, only to find that the opposing insurance company's attorney has Facebook photos of the plaintiff water-skiing and horseback riding! Again, those photos could be used in court.

What you post can even come into play after your case settles. For example, the daughter of a plaintiff in an age-discrimination lawsuit cost her father an $80,000 settlement. She made a Facebook post that discussed specifics of the case, violating the confidentiality clause that was part of the settlement. Some of her "friends" leaked the post. The opposing lawyers used her mistake against the plantiff and won. Her father lost the $80,000 settlement.

Many Facebook users have a false sense of security that only their approved "friends" will see the information they post. However, many people do not set their security levels to the highest settings. Also, no one can stop your "friends" from sharing the information with others.

Everything you do online leaves an electronic trail that can be difficult, or sometimes impossible, to erase. Think about this before you post! When involved in legal proceedings, don't disclose anything about your case on social media. It's not worth it.

CHAPTER 19
Time Limitations

From the moment your car crashed, the clock began to tick on your case. Like most legal rights, auto accident personal injury claims have strict deadlines. Some time limitations are well known. For example, you probably already realize that you could lose all rights against the driver who caused your accident and the responsible insurance company if you fail to file a lawsuit against them within a year of the accident.

In most states, the deadline by which you must file your lawsuit is known as the statute of limitation. However, in Louisiana, the term used is *prescription*. Essentially, prescription is the time in which you must file suit before your claim will no longer be viable. This brief section will discuss the prescription time for most suits

> **FAST FACT**
> Most personal injury lawsuits must be filed within one year of the auto accident.

that you will encounter for personal injury cases. It is important to note that if you decide to sue, it is not always advantageous to wait until the end of the prescriptive period. Prescription is a deadline, not a suggestion.

NEGLIGENCE/OTHER TORTS

Though prescription varies from issue to issue in the law, prescription for most causes of action from an automobile accident will be one year. In other words, you will have to decide to file a lawsuit and contact your lawyer early enough so that your attorney still has time to draft and file a lawsuit within one year. This year period commences to run from the day of the automobile accident. Therefore, you have time to decide whether you want to sue, but you do not have an unlimited amount of time. One year is usually the limit of time you have in personal injury cases.

WRONGFUL DEATH

If you have the unfortunate experience of having a loved one die as a result of a car accident, you may be able to bring a wrongful death lawsuit in order to recover damages that you have experienced from that person's death. This includes damages for monetary as well as intangible support. You must bring this action within one year of the automobile accident victim's death (rather than the date of the accident).

SURVIVAL ACTION

Again, if you have the unfortunate experience of having a loved one killed by an automobile accident, you may be able to also bring a survival action lawsuit. Essentially, you are suing in the place of the victim of the car accident for the personal injuries of that victim. There are two prescriptive periods for a survival action lawsuit. The standard prescriptive time for this lawsuit is one year after the automobile accident occurs. However, if the victim survives the accident but dies before a year passes from the accident, then this period restarts and you have one year from the death of the victim.

CHAPTER 20
Insurance Coverage

As a driver, there are several things you should understand regarding Louisiana's auto insurance laws. It is important to be compliant with the auto insurance laws, and the state's auto liability insurance coverage minimum requirements. Vehicle owners and operators who are uninsured can be subject to penalties, fines, and the impoundment of their vehicles. If you do not carry liability insurance, you are also at risk of being personally responsible for costs associated with any accidents for which you are at fault.

Additionally, what many people do not know is that Louisiana has a "no pay, no play" insurance law which prohibits someone from pursuing some damages from another person's insurance company if they do not have auto insurance of their own. This means if you are in an auto accident, even if the accident is not your fault, you may not be able to recover the cost to repair your vehicle or pay your medical expenses if you do not have auto insurance. People without an insurance policy, obviously, do not have an insurance company of their own from which they can recover. The upshot is that those without auto insurance can be left with a huge property loss and much more, no matter which person was at fault in their accident. The best way to protect yourself before an accident is to purchase as much uninsured motorist (UM) coverage as possible.

AUTO INSURANCE REQUIREMENTS

Louisiana law requires that a person carry liability insurance coverage on any vehicle he or she owns. Liability insurance covers the damage to another person's property and the costs of another person's bodily injuries caused by the owner of a vehicle or anyone driving the vehicle with the owner's permission. It also covers damages caused by any person listed on the policy when driving someone else's vehicle as well. It is important to note that every vehicle in Louisiana must be individually insured, not just the owner and driver. If a person owns more than one vehicle, they must all be listed on the policy, or otherwise insured, as well the normal drivers of those vehicles.

> **FAST FACT**
> Liability insurance covers injuries and property damage you cause other people.

Liability coverage pays for damage caused by the driver of the insured vehicle up to the insurance policy's pre-set limits. The amount of insurance coverage a person decides to have on his or her policy can vary greatly. Almost every state, however, sets by law the required minimum liability coverage limit that all vehicles must carry to be registered in that state.

The minimum liability coverage required by law in Louisiana must include at least the following:

- $15,000 coverage for bodily injury to any one person,
- $30,000 coverage for total bodily injury for all people per accident, and
- $25,000 coverage for property damage (*e.g.*, damage to a vehicle).

This state-required minimum coverage is often referred to as the 15/30/25 requirement. It is important to make sure you have at least the minimum required liability coverage on all of your vehicles. Uninsured motorists can be subject to penalties, fines, fees, and other sanctions just for not carrying the required amount of coverage. Drivers who cannot provide proof of valid insurance can have their automobiles impounded and fees assessed until insurance is provided. Also, proof of insurance is required to complete most DMV transactions, such as obtaining a license or vehicle registration. If not having proof of insurance is preventing someone from obtaining a valid driver's license or vehicle registration, that person is only subjecting him- or herself to additional fines, fees, and penalties.

Additionally, if you do not carry any liability coverage, you are at risk of being personally responsible for all of the costs and expenses of any damages you cause in an accident. This means that if you are in an auto accident and have no insurance, then you likely will have to pay out of your own pocket for all of the repair costs and medical expenses you cause to another person, no matter how big or small they are. Regardless of a person's financial situation, the state minimum coverage is established to be affordable for all individuals, and one should refrain from operating a vehicle if it cannot be obtained.

OTHER TYPES OF INSURANCE COVERAGE

Although 15/30/25 is the amount of liability insurance coverage required by law, it is a good idea to have an insurance policy that has more coverage than this if possible. If you are at fault in an accident where the cost of the accident exceeds your policy limits, you can be personally responsible for any costs above that amount. Since costs of an auto accident can sometimes be great, this means that if you are underinsured, you are still at a great risk of being personally responsible for a portion of the huge costs associated with an auto accident every time you operate a vehicle.

Let's say that Jack was at fault in an accident that resulted in Greg's going to the hospital, and Jack only had the state-required minimum coverage. Jack could be personally responsible for any hospital expenses that Greg has above $15,000. Depending on the severity of the injury, Greg's hospital bill could easily exceed $15,000, especially when you consider the high cost of medical expenses. The same goes for the damage to Greg's vehicle. If Greg drove a $50,000 BMW that was totaled because of the accident, Jack could be responsible for any damages above his policy limit of $25,000. These numbers are if only one car and one injured person were involved. If you are at fault in a multi-car accident, you can be looking at serious amounts of money. When you think about all of the costs associated with an auto accident, such as medical bills, car repairs, etc., the state-required minimum coverage is often not enough to cover all of these expenses. If you are held personally responsible for the additional costs, you will have to pay the money out of your own pocket.

It is also important to be aware that the state requires only liability insurance. This means that the law only requires you to carry insurance for the damage you or the driver of your vehicle cause to another person or another person's property. Depending on your situation, it may be a good idea to have other types of insurance coverage, such as comprehensive and collision insurance. **Comprehensive coverage** pays for the cost of damage to your own vehicle that occurs as a result of a non-collision incident, such as fire, flood, theft, falling objects, or vandalism. **Collision coverage** pays for damages to your own automobile caused by collision with another vehicle or object when YOU are at fault for the accident (or if the person at fault does not pay). Liability-only insurance, which is all that is required by the state, will not pay to fix your vehicle when you were the individual at fault for the accident. It also could be a good idea to get **uninsured/underinsured (UM) motorist coverage**. This insurance coverage pays expenses including your personal injury damages when a driver who has no insurance, or too little insurance to pay for the full amount of your damages, hits you. Although the law does not require all of these types of coverage, it is a good idea to talk to an insurance agent and see what might be needed for your situation.

LOUISIANA'S "NO PAY, NO PLAY" LAW

Another big reason it is important to carry the state-required minimum liability insurance coverage is Louisiana's "no pay, no play" law. This law makes it more difficult for a person to recover damages related to their auto accident from another person's insurance company if they do not have an auto insurance policy themselves. The "no pay, no play" law does not allow uninsured motorists to collect the first $15,000 in personal injuries and the first $25,000 in property damages, regardless of who was at fault in the accident.

Louisiana has one of the highest uninsured motorist rates in the country. Generally, high numbers of uninsured motorists also mean high insurance costs. This is because when someone without insurance coverage causes an accident, that person does not have an insurance plan to pay their costs. Normally, the driver not at fault would receive money for damages from his or her own insurance company, which would in turn collect the money from the at-fault person's insurance company. If the person at fault does not have insurance, the insurance company for the person who was not at fault must seek to collect those funds directly from the at-fault driver. If they are not successful, which frequently happens, those costs are passed along to the consumer in the form of higher insurance premiums for everyone.

In an attempt to lower the cost of insurance premiums in the state and reduce the number of uninsured drivers, Louisiana has adopted the "no pay, no play" law prohibiting those without insurance from recovering costs for the first $15,000 in personal injuries damages and $25,000 in property damage they would otherwise have received from an auto accident.

> **FAST FACT**
> If you drive without insurance, Louisiana's "no pay, no play" law may prevent you from recovering money for your damages.

This may not seem significant, but let's say Bill drives a truck worth $20,000, and Carl hit him and was at fault for the accident. If Bill's truck was totally destroyed, but he was driving without auto insurance, he would not be reimbursed for any amount of money for his damaged truck, since he cannot recover for the first $25,000 in property damage. Bill does not have auto insurance to pay for the cost of damages to others when he is at fault, and already can be personally responsible for those costs. Under Louisiana's "no pay, no play" law, he will also not be able to recover his own costs when someone else is at fault. This law imposes a harsh reality on those who choose to drive without auto insurance.

It is important to realize that you only need to have the state-required liability insurance and not full coverage to be able to recover from another person's insurance company. Without collision insurance, you will still not be able to recover for damage to your vehicle when you are at fault, but it is important to at least obtain the state-required liability insurance so you won't be negatively affected by this law.

There are a few limitations to keep in mind about the "no pay, no play" law, however. The law does not apply if the driver at fault was intoxicated at the time of the accident or fled the scene of the accident. Even if someone does not have any auto insurance, he or she can still file claims against another individual's insurance in the case of a drunk-driving or hit-and-run accident. This law also does not apply to legally parked cars, even if the parked car was uninsured. Additionally, it does not apply to uninsured drivers from other states, though they can still be cited for driving without insurance and face other serious penalties and fines.

Although additional insurance coverage is highly recommended, drivers should always carry at least the state-required minimum liability auto insurance coverage on all of their vehicles. No matter one's financial situation, the minimum coverage is set at an amount to be reasonably affordable for everyone. A person should refrain from driving if he or she is not able to obtain this minimum coverage. There are several resources available to consumers on how to obtain affordable car insurance. A person puts him or herself at risk of severe penalties, fines, fees, great amounts of property loss, and personal injury costs without it.

CHAPTER 21
Mediation and Arbitration

Once it is established that an individual has a valid personal injury case against another party, there are many different ways to bring the case to resolution. Although our judicial system in the United States is what most people are familiar with, bringing a case to court is not the only way people can seek to have a dispute resolved. Alternative Dispute Resolution (ADR) is a general term encompassing various techniques for resolving conflict outside of court using a neutral third party. In the case of an auto accident, usually the dispute needing resolution is: who is at fault in the accident, and for what amount of damages? This can be accomplished in different ways, and two of the most common ADR methods used in auto accident personal injury cases are mediation and arbitration.

If someone has been injured in an auto accident, that person is seeking to recover damages from another party. Whether it is from an individual or company, the most commonly-known way to recover those damages is to sue that party in the court of law. Generally when suing someone in court system, the case goes to trial in front of a judge, and possibly a jury. At that time both parties will present their evidence, witnesses, and interpretation of the facts and events that unfolded surrounding the accident. A judge or jury will decide the outcome of the case, including who was at fault, to what extent they were at fault, and what amount of damages, if any, should be awarded to each side. This process of taking a case to trial can be very lengthy and expensive for both sides, sometimes taking years to resolve the matter. This means that even if one party was fully at fault in an auto accident, it could be years before those who were injured or damaged in the accident may be able to receive any actual money from that person.

It is for this reason that many cases are resolved outside of the courtroom, before the case ever goes to trial. For the purpose of efficiency of both time and money, many cases never actually see the courtroom floor. Alternative Dispute Resolution is an alternative to the court system. Sometimes cases will be started in court and be resolved before going to trial, or a case may never be filed in court at all. How a case becomes resolved depends on the circumstances, but as stated before the two most important alternative dispute resolution methods to be aware of are mediation and arbitration.

> **FAST FACT**
>
> Many auto accident personal injury cases never go to court and are resolved by the ADR process of mediation.

Mediation is a non-binding method of dispute resolution wherein a mediator facilitates communication between the opposing parties in an effort for them to come to a mutual agreement on how to resolve the case. The mediator's job is to be a neutral third party that helps guide negotiations and settlement between the parties. In many cases, a mediator will be able to help the parties decide on a mutually agreeable amount of damages to be paid by one party to the other, without having to bring the case to trial. That is to say, instead of taking the case to court where a judge and jury will decide on the outcome of the case, the parties will come to an agreement on the outcome themselves. If the mediation process does not work, and the parties are not able to agree, they still have the option of litigating the matter in court.

Arbitration, on the other hand, is a process in which the parties agree to submit their case to an independent arbitrator for evaluation, and must adhere to the decision the arbitrator makes about their case. An arbitrator is similar in some ways to a judge. He or she is an independent third party that reviews the evidence in the case and gives a decision that is legally binding on both sides. In this way, an arbitrator is much more similar to a judge than a mediator because, as with a judge, the parties must adhere to the arbitrator's ruling. However, this process is still much faster and more efficient than bringing the case to trial because, unlike with a judge, the parties do not have the right to appeal the arbitrator's ruling.

Both mediation and arbitration can avoid the formalities, delays, and expenses of ordinary litigation. An injured party may be able to recover money more quickly than with in-court litigation. Since the parties cannot appeal the decision of an arbitrator like they could with a judge, it saves both sides the time and money of possible lengthy appeals. If the case is successfully mediated, the parties can come to an agreement much faster than battling the matter in court. Because of this, the cost and expenses of resolving the case in this manner are often much less. There are also some risks involved in these processes, so it is important to understand how mediation and arbitration work, and how they apply to auto accident personal injury cases specifically.

> **FAST FACT**
> Mediation results in the injured party receiving money for his or her damages much more quickly than trial would allow.

MEDIATION

Mediation is the ADR technique most commonly used to resolve auto accident personal injury cases. Mediation is an informal negotiation process that is used to resolve disputes, which is facilitated by the help of an independent mediator. The parties meet with a neutral mediator in an attempt to mutually resolve their dispute. The mediator has no decision-making authority. Instead, he or she is there to help the parties clarify issues, explore settlement options, and evaluate how to advance each side's particular interests. The purpose of mediation is to help the opposing parties communicate and understand each other's positions with the hope of reaching an agreement that satisfies both sides. In mediation there is no third party, such as a judge or jury, which decides the matter. The parties involved either come to the agreement on the outcome of the case with the help of the mediator, or fail to resolve the matter and return the case to court.

Mediation is usually a voluntary process, but a court may—and often will—order the parties to attempt mediation. Although a court can force parties to attend mediation sessions, it cannot force them to come to an agreement. Since the mediation process only results in a binding agreement on a party when the party agrees to it, there are very few drawbacks to at least attempting mediation. Usually parties will first attempt to negotiate a settlement on their own, but often agree to mediate the case (even where a judge does not order it) in an attempt to save the time and expenses of going to trial if their negotiations fail. If the parties are still unable to come an agreement after mediation, the alternative option of going to trial on the matter is always still available. Whether voluntary or ordered by a judge, the following five elements are key to understanding the mediation process.

The Role of the Mediator

The mediator is a neutral third party who has usually had specific training on the mediation process, how to assist parties in reaching agreements, and how to bring disputes to settlement. The mediator is not a judge and is not there to give legal advice on the case. He or she cannot make decisions for the parties or give recommendations related to the proposed agreement. The mediator's job is simply to help facilitate the agreement and to get both sides to arrive at a solution that meets everyone's needs and works for both parties.

Mediators are usually attorneys or retired judges. Some are full-time mediators and no longer represent clients, while others only work part time as mediators. Whether or not they are still actively representing clients, they usually have expertise in the area of law that they are mediating. Many mediators in auto accident personal injury cases are attorneys who have previously practiced, or still currently practice, in that area of law. If a judge orders the case for mediation, the parties usually have the opportunity to mutually agree on the person to be appointed as the mediator. However, if they cannot agree, the court will appoint one. The mediator's job is to primarily act as a buffer between the two parties during negotiations. He or she will not take sides, as the mediator's job is not to determine a winner or loser, but to merely facilitate communication between the sides.

Who Will Be There and How It Works

Both parties and their attorneys will need to be present at the mediation session. Anyone else whom the parties feel they need to consult with, such as a spouse or parent, before agreeing to settle their case should also plan to be present. Although the opposing attorney will be at the mediation, the defendant driver or responsible party may not be present, depending on the situation. Either way, someone from the opposing party's insurance company will likely attend or be available. Oftentimes the payment for damages will come from the opposing party's insurance company, so they will have a great deal of input on how much they are willing to pay in settlement of the case. If the person seeking damages was injured in the accident, then a representative from his or her health insurance company may attend the mediation or be available as well, because the health insurance company will also have an interest in the outcome of the case.

Usually mediations take place in conference rooms at the mediator's office, or in a similar location, where both sides can get together and present their case. The mediator will begin with an introduction in which he or she will explain the mediation process and any other relevant rules. Both sides are then given the opportunity to present their case, including any evidence and exhibits they may have. After this, the parties will separate and sit in different rooms. At this point, the mediator usually goes back and forth between the parties to try to negotiate a settlement agreement. The mediator may point out potential weaknesses in parties' cases or other relevant issues. This is a helpful step in the process, because the parties involved should understand the weaknesses in their case and the risks of going to trial. The mediator will spend time talking to each side about the case, including information about the person's injuries and damages.

It is important to understand that at this point in the process, the parties are usually trying to negotiate the amount of money to be paid by one party to the other. That is to say, if a case has reached mediation, one party has probably already accepted the reality of paying damages to the other side, and are merely negotiating over the amount that is to be paid. Each party can make settlement offers, and the parties can explain to the mediator what they feel may help them to achieve settlement. If the participants are able to reach an agreement in mediation, they will sign a written settlement

> **FAST FACT**
> Mediation is a confidential process. Nothing said or done during mediation can be used against you if your case goes to trial.

document, and if not the case will continue in court as it would have otherwise.

Most clients find it reassuring to know that everything said in mediation is confidential. None of the oral and written communications and records may be used as evidence in any future judicial proceeding. In effect, if the parties do not end up agreeing on a settlement and the case instead goes back to court, things that are said or done in the mediation process cannot later be used against the parties. This is because the law is set up to encourage people to settle matters outside of the judicial system if possible. For this reason, the law protects information given in the mediation, so that both parties can feel free to express any and all information that can help effectuate settlement without fear of recourse in later proceedings. Therefore, all parties should be ready to talk about whatever matters they feel will help move the case towards settlement.

How to Prepare for Mediation

Both parties should be prepared for the process to take a long time. The mediation process can take anywhere from a few hours to a full day—and, in rare exceptions, several days. Getting both sides of a dispute to voluntarily agree to a solution that works for all the parties involved is not usually an easy task and can take time. Both sides should be prepared to be patient with the mediation process and to allow for the negotiations to run their course.

If any parties were injured in the auto accident, they should be prepared to tell the mediator about the pain, discomfort, and physical problems from which they are suffering. They should also be prepared to talk about their work, household, and family situations and how they have been affected by the injuries from the accident. If there is any other relevant information that will affect the settlement, they should be prepared to talk about that as well. However, those who were injured are not required to talk. It is quite common for them to let their lawyers do all the talking.

Most importantly, parties should be prepared to compromise. If the parties' goal is to reach a settlement, they will likely have to compromise on what they expect to receive. It is important to remember, though, that a settlement is not a victory or a defeat. The injured parties may not get everything they would if they won at trial, but they also don't risk being defeated at trial and getting nothing. A reasonable settlement amount will likely fall somewhere in between a "best day at trial" and "worst day at trial" scenario. At mediation, the parties can control the outcome, as opposed to trial where the judge or jury will decide. Jury trials can be very uncertain, and sometimes the same case can be tried before two different juries and have two completely different outcomes. Settlement is not a win or loss, but an alternate resolution to trial that has many advantages. However, settlement may involve giving up some of what a party wants in order to achieve resolution.

> **FAST FACT**
> At mediation, the parties can control the outcome, as opposed to trial where the judge or jury will decide.

Before mediation starts, a party and his or her attorney should discuss what level of compromise they find acceptable. Even if an amount was discussed, they should still be prepared to be flexible if the circumstances warrant it. Expect offers from the opposing side that seem far from what you expect, especially in the beginning. It is important to be patient and let the negotiation process unfold. It most cases, the parties can eventually reach an amount that works for both sides, as long as they remain calm, level-headed, and patient.

The Settlement Process

If a person is trying to recover damages from another party, one of the big advantages of mediation is the ability to receive his or her money much sooner. If a case is settled in mediation, a person can possibly get his or her money in a matter of weeks. If the case is not settled at mediation, one could wait years before getting paid—assuming that one wins at all. In addition to receiving the money more quickly, settlement allows for the stress of the lawsuit to be over that much sooner, and for both sides to be able to move on with their lives.

As discussed before, it is important to remember that a settlement is not a victory or a defeat. A settlement at mediation can often results in more money actually going to the injured party, even when a trial would result in a higher amount being awarded, because of all of the costs and fees associated with trial. In other words, even if the amount awarded at trial was bigger than the amount paid at mediation, the amount actually received by the injured party can be lower. Bringing a case to trial can be expensive because of costs for things such as depositions, testimony, and witness subpoenas that are needed to in order to try a case in court. Court costs and attorney's fees can also add up over extended litigation, which can come out of the amount awarded to the injured party. Additionally, insurers that have made payment for medical bills or other expenses and are entitled to reimbursement will often reduce the amount of their reimbursement claim when cases are settled. If a case is taken to trial, those amounts often must be paid in full. For these reasons, even if one could be

> **FAST FACT**
> Settling your case at mediation—even for even a smaller amount—could result in more money in your pocket than a larger jury verdict, due to the high cost of litigation and the value of the time required to endure a trial.

awarded more at trial than is being offered at mediation, it is very likely that the injured party could both end up with more money and receive the money sooner with a settlement. These are important factors to keep in mind when deciding whether to accept a settlement offer at mediation.

That being said, one of the reasons why the attendance of the parties in mediation is required is because an attorney cannot enter into a settlement agreement without the authorization of his or her client. No matter what the attorney's recommendation might be—which often may be not to accept settlement—it must be the client's decision whether or not to accept a settlement offer. For this reason, it is important that the injured party understands all of the risks and benefits of accepting a settlement agreement.

If the parties successfully settle the case at mediation, the mediator will prepare a settlement agreement for all parties to sign. The executed written agreement will dispose of the dispute, and that agreement will create an enforceable contract. The agreement will likely include a confidentiality agreement, meaning the parties cannot disclose the terms of the agreement to anyone else. It is important to note that even posting any information about a settlement agreement on social media sites would be a breach of confidentiality and will void the settlement agreement. Confidentiality agreements are in place to protect both sides, and any public or private conveyance of this information would violate the agreement.

If the mediation results in an impasse, the lawsuit will continue as if the mediation never occurred. However, this is not the only chance for settlement. Both sides can revisit the possibility of settlement when trial approaches, or at any other time on their own. Sometimes parties will even agree to attempt mediation a second time. However, you should not expect that the case will necessarily settle at some point down the road if it fails at mediation, because mediation is usually the best chance for it to happen.

The Advantages of Mediation

There are several advantages to at least attempting mediation. For one thing, the parties have no commitment to settle the case on the outset. If the parties are not able to come to an agreement they are both happy with, litigation will continue as if mediation were never attempted. Therefore, there is little harm in attempting mediation when the parties believe that an agreement between them could be possible.

Assuming an agreement can be reached, the following are some of the advantages of mediation:

- Mediation can help protect privacy since it is a confidential process, unlike courtroom proceedings that are open to the public.
- If the parties agree to settle, the injured party will usually get the funds within a few weeks, as opposed to several months or possibly years later.
- The parties involved make the decision, not a judge or jury, which gives them more control over the outcome.
- Having a case decided in mediation may mean lower attorney fees and costs.
- Both parties can avoid the stress and uncertainty involved in a drawn-out lawsuit that can take years to resolve.
- If an agreement is not reached in mediation, the case can still be decided by a jury or resolved in some other way.
- Even if parties decide not to settle the case, what happened and was said during mediation is confidential and cannot be brought into court.

It is important to understand the process and have realistic expectations about what the results of mediation will be. Although an injured party may have to compromise on the amount of money being awarded, if both parties can come to an agreement on an amount that seems reasonable, the injured party will receive his or her money more quickly, can avoid a drawn-out legal battle, won't risk the chance of not being awarded any damages at trial, and—because of the cost savings of avoiding litigation—may come out with more money at the end of the day.

ARBITRATION

Arbitration is an Alternative Dispute Resolution (ADR) process which, unlike mediation, allows an agreed-upon person to hear evidence and decide the outcome in a way similar to how a judge would in court. Just like mediation, this dispute resolution process is done outside of the court system and can result in the matter being resolved much faster than if the case had to be decided in court. The biggest difference, however, is that the parties in arbitration do not come to a mutual agreement on the case. Although parties may voluntarily decide to enter arbitration, it is the arbitrator who decides the outcome of the case, and not the parties themselves. Additionally, once the parties agree to enter the arbitration process, they are bound by the arbitrator's decision, even if it is not in one party's best interest. This means even if one party is not pleased with the outcome of the case, that person does not have the right to challenge it in court unless he or she agreed ahead of time to only non-binding arbitration, except under extreme circumstances. However, there are still many advantages to arbitration over the normal judicial system.

In a car accident case, an arbitrator will decide a number of key questions—such as the question of whether one party will recover money damages from the other driver, and if so, how much that party will recover. Because these questions are decided in a single arbitration session and cannot be appealed, it usually saves both parties a great deal of time and money when compared to taking a case to court. Sometimes, especially in car accident cases, it might be better to get the opposing party to agree to arbitration because, unlike with mediation, you will be assured of a resolution at the end of the process. Just because parties agree to mediation does not mean they will come to any resolution on the matter. Arbitration, on the other hand, ensures that the case will be resolved one way or the other. If an injured party is confident that he or she is entitled to some amount of damages, then getting the opposing side to agree to arbitration may be the fastest way to achieve a favorable result.

The Arbitration Process

An arbitration session is usually more formal than mediation, but less so than a courtroom proceeding. Like mediation, it is usually conducted in an office or conference room. However, arbitration is far less common than mediation in motor vehicle accident bodily injury cases. The arbitrator makes a decision about the case based upon the evidence presented and the testimony of the parties and witnesses. The length of the actual arbitration session depends on the complexity of the case, but the total length of the process is much shorter then taking a case to trial; however, in many ways an arbitration session is similar to a trial setting. Each side presents their evidence and version of the facts as they see them, and witnesses for both sides will testify under oath. Many times the formal rules of evidence will not apply, or the parties will agree ahead of time on a limited version of the rules of evidence. This means that the arbitrator can consider evidence that would otherwise not be admissible in court. This could either work for or against a party's favor, and is something that each party's attorney must consider when deciding if the arbitration process would be advantageous for his or her client.

The arbitrator can be a retired judge, an experienced lawyer, or anyone else that the two parties can agree upon, but usually arbitrators are individuals who have specialized their legal career in the arbitration process. Arbitration is usually conducted through independent private companies that are members of the American Arbitration Association. Once the parties have agreed to arbitration, they will have to agree upon who the arbitrator will be. Additionally, they must agree on whether the arbitrator's decision will be binding or non-binding. If the parties agree that the arbitrator's decision is binding, then the arbitrator's decision is final and cannot be appealed. By doing this, the parties are agreeing that they will they be bound by the arbitrator's decision no matter the outcome. In a non-binding arbitration, the arbitrator can recommend a decision, but it cannot be forced on either party. A non-binding arbitration can be beneficial because it can give the parties a chance to see how a neutral third party, such as a judge or jury, might rule on the case. This can help facilitate an agreement or settlement between the parties at a later time. If a non-binding arbitration fails to resolve the case, then the parties still retain the option of going forward with trial. Parties also have the option of only arbitrating certain issues, or agreeing to what is known as "high-low" arbitration.

Sometimes parties will agree to a limited arbitration process where the arbitrator only decides one or two issues instead of the entire case. For example, the parties may agree on who is at fault in the accident, but disagree as to the value of the damages. In that case, the parties may arbitrate only the valuation of damages aspect of the case. That means the arbitrator will only decide what amount should be awarded, and nothing else.

They may also agree to what is known as a "high-low" arbitration provision. In high-low arbitration, there is an agreement ahead of time as to a minimum and maximum award amount, no matter what the arbitrator decides. Usually, the arbitrator does not know of this agreement. This means, for example, that if the parties agree to a low amount of $15,000 and a high of $50,000 and the arbitrator awarded $0 in damages to the injured party, then the injured party would still receive $15,000. On the other hand, if the arbitrator awarded damages of $100,000, the injured person would instead only receive the agreed-upon maximum of $50,000. This ensures that the injured party will receive some amount of damages, but caps the maximum that will have to be paid by the other party. This is done to protect the interests of both sides. By agreeing to cap the maximum amount of damages, the injured party can make certain that he or she will not walk away empty handed, or with much less than the amount to which he or she feels entitled. This method can be used when parties are attempting to settle a dispute, but cannot agree on the exact amount of damages to be paid.

Advantages of Arbitration

Although the decision to submit to arbitration is usually voluntary on both sides, it can be an extremely useful method of resolving a dispute, especially when it comes to auto accident personal injury cases.

The following are advantages to resolving auto accident personal injury cases through arbitration.

1. **It is less expensive than trial.** Unlike ligation, which can have many hearing and trial dates that have court costs associated with each of them, arbitration requires a one-time, relatively low fee.

2. **It is faster than trial.** In litigation, a trial can drag out for years. Arbitration can usually be scheduled within a few weeks or months of the parties' agreement to arbitrate, and will occur on one occasion, after which the case will be resolved.
3. **It is less stressful than trial.** Arbitration offers a more informal environment than trial. Since it can be scheduled, there is also less waiting around, and fewer formalities as well.
4. **It allows the parties to have a "high-low" agreement.** As mentioned earlier, this type of agreement ensures that the injured person will not walk away empty handed. With a high-low agreement, the attorneys have previously agreed upon an allowed range of damages. This type of agreement is not available at trial.
5. **It provides for greater predictability.** Since an arbitrator is a trained attorney and is selected by the involved parties, he or she is more likely to understand the law and value of the case. A jury can be unpredictable, and often returns drastically inconsistent verdicts.
6. **The rules of evidence are relaxed.** As previously discussed, many times the formal rules of evidence will not apply, or the parties will agree ahead of time on a limited version of the evidence rules. This means that the arbitrator can consider evidence that would otherwise not be admissible in court. This could work in one party's favor, and is something that party's attorney may consider advantageous.
7. **The parties can mutually agree on the arbitration process.** When deciding on various aspects of the arbitration process, the parties can work together on these decisions. This allows them more flexibility and input in the process than they would have at trial, where the judge and jury make all of the decisions.

Arbitration can be a good alternative to taking a case to trial in certain circumstances. Arbitration can create a legally binding decision and more quickly result in a satisfactory outcome to the case. It is important to consult with an attorney to consider the advantages and disadvantages of mediation or arbitration, and to decide if either may be a good method of resolution for your case.

CHAPTER 22
The Discovery Process

The discovery phase of your lawsuit occurs after you have filed a petition in court and the opposing party has filed an answer. Discovery occurs before your case goes to trial. When we think of lawsuits as we see them on television, we often think of our attorney finding the "smoking gun" that will win our case, and presenting this to a witness on the stand while catching them in a lie. In reality, surprising the opposing party with a "smoking gun" rarely occurs, if ever. This is a result of the discovery process.

> **FAST FACT**
> Discovery is the compulsory disclosure of information at the request of an opposing party.

Discovery occurs when both parties to a lawsuit turn over information that is related to the suit. It is an exchange of valuable information. Discovery is very broad; both parties can ask about any matter relevant to the lawsuit. While it may be frustrating to have to answer so many detailed questions during discovery, this process is very beneficial. Discovery allows attorneys to develop the strongest argument for their case using all the information available, which then allows a judge or jury to fairly decide whose argument has the most merit. There are many tools that a lawyer uses to learn information about the case throughout the discovery process, such as interrogatories, requests for production of documents, requests for admission, subpoenas, and depositions.

INTERROGATORIES

The most common discovery tool used to gain information is the interrogatory. Interrogatories are a set of questions submitted by the opposing attorney for you to answer. It allows the opposing lawyer to learn more about you and the basis of your lawsuit. Your lawyer will first read the questions to determine if anything is unanswerable because it is covered by a privilege, such as the attorney-client privilege. If nothing is covered by a privilege, your attorney will then provide you with the questions to answer.

The questions will vary, but interrogatories will ask for all of your basic information, such as your birthday, Social Security number, phone number, address and previous addresses, employment, spousal information, etc. In many situations, you fill out paperwork when you hire your lawyer that answers many of the questions provided in interrogatories. Your lawyer will then answer the interrogatories for you using information you have already provided to him or her. The interrogatories that ask for your basic information are expected and are easily answered.

Interrogatories can become more of a burden when you are asked more detailed, private information. This includes things such as your medical history, employment history, salary, any government aid received, other lawsuits you may have been involved in, and even criminal history. The opposing attorney can ask about this information because it may be relevant to the lawsuit. For example, you may have a claim that your neck was injured in the car accident. The opposing attorney has a right to know if you had prior problems with your neck that were aggravated, rather than caused, by the car accident. Your lawyer is there to help you answer the interrogatories honestly and professionally, because your answers are admissible as evidence in your trial. However, it is okay if you do not know all of the answers to interrogatories—they can be changed later. If you answer an interrogatory and later remember more details or need to change your answer, you can notify your attorney and he or she can amend the interrogatory. There is usually a limit to the number of interrogatories the opposing lawyer is allowed to ask, so the number of questions will not be excessive. Interrogatories are the most useful tool lawyers use to learn more about you and your lawsuit, and this process helps deliver the fairest result in a case.

REQUESTS FOR PRODUCTION OF DOCUMENTS

Another discovery tool used to gain information is requests for the production of documents. The opposing attorney will often attach document requests to interrogatories. Requests for production of documents are written requests by the opposing attorney that you provide documents for his or her inspection or copying. After you answer your interrogatories, you will then be required to send these documents or copies of documents to the opposing attorney.

Requests for production of documents typically include your driver's license, copies of your motor vehicle insurance card, vehicle registration, and health insurance card. The opposing attorney will request a copy of the accident report. If you took any pictures of your motor vehicle accident, you will have to provide copies of the pictures. You will also have to provide copies of your medical records. This usually amounts to a large stack of papers, so your attorney will get all of these documents from you, copy them, and compile the documents to be sent to the opposing attorney. This makes the discovery process more organized and efficient.

REQUESTS FOR ADMISSION

Rather than ask for information through interrogatories, the opposing lawyer may request for an admission. Requests for admission are written requests that you admit or deny a specific fact or the truthfulness of a document. This is usually the last discovery tool used before trial. Lawyers use this to clear up facts that they do not want to have to discuss during trial. For example, you may be asked to admit that you took the photograph of your vehicle bumper on July 5, 2012. When you admit this information, it saves time during trial because the attorney will not have to ask you this information again. There is no limit to the number of requests for admission that an attorney may ask of you, which makes requests for admission different from interrogatories.

SUBPEONAS

Subpoenas are used by the court to aid attorneys in the discovery process. A subpoena as used in the trial context is a written order commanding a person to appear in court and testify. A subpoena during the discovery process is different. A subpoena in discovery is a written order commanding a person to make a sworn statement at a specific time and place, other than a trial. The person gives his or her sworn statement through a deposition. Subpoenas can also be used to compel non-parties to the lawsuit to provide documents. If you are a party to the lawsuit, you provide documents through requests for production. If you need documents from a business or person who is not a party to the lawsuit, you subpoena them. For example, the automobile repair shop that fixed your vehicle may be subpoenaed to provide the document detailing all of the damage and the repair price.

DEPOSITIONS

A deposition is out-of-court testimony. After your interrogatory answers are received, the opposing attorney will ask for your deposition. This discovery tool occurs when parties agree on a time and place where you will give a sworn statement and be asked questions. Both attorneys are present at the deposition. Your statement is recorded by a court reporter and transcribed on a document as admissible evidence to be used in trial. Depositions typically occur at your attorney's office and take a few hours. You will be asked all of your basic information, as well as information about the accident, the time leading up to the accident, the medical attention you received, and the effects of the accident. Your attorney is there to object to any questions the opposing attorney asks that are inappropriate. A subpoena is not needed to get a deposition from a party to the lawsuit. Instead, to depose a party, your lawyer will serve a notice of deposition. On the other hand, a subpoena is often required to get a deposition from a non-party.

CHAPTER 23
Wrongful Death and Survival Claims

Losing a family member due to another person's fault is always tragic. As an auto accident attorney, the most sensitive aspect of my law practice is helping clients handle the horrors of losing a loved one in a car crash. It is weighty, gut-wrenching work.

For example, a few years ago I represented a grieving family in a case involving the heartbreaking death of a 12-year-old boy on his bicycle caused by a speeding pizza delivery driver. Of course, I cannot begin to comprehend how difficult this tragedy has been for his surviving parents and grandparents. Their lives were changed forever in an instant. They never got to say goodbye, or watch him grow up to achieve his dream of becoming a police officer.

The sudden loss of a loved one due to another person's fault can leave surviving family members feeling understandably angry, confused, depressed, financially unstable, helpless, and utterly alone. Although the legal system obviously cannot bring back the deceased, a successful wrongful death case could at least help the surviving family members process the pain and get back on their feet by holding the responsible party accountable.

Successful representation in a death case begins with a careful explanation of the legal nature of the claims.

Louisiana law recognizes two different actions that arise out of a death caused by another person's fault: 1) survival action, and 2) wrongful death action.

A **survival action** permits recovery for those damages suffered by the deceased victim from the time of injury to the moment of his or her death. The elements of damages for a survival action are pain and suffering, loss of earnings, and other damages sustained by the victim up to the moment of death, such as fright, fear, or mental anguish while the deadly ordeal was in progress.

> **FAST FACT**
> Survival actions address damages suffered by the deceased victim from the time of injury to the moment of death.

A **wrongful death action**, on the other hand, is intended to compensate surviving family members for their suffering and loss after death. The elements of damage for a wrongful death action are loss of love, affection, companionship, and support, and funeral expenses.

Wrongful death damages are in addition to personal injury damages, and are owed to the family for the loss of their loved one when a person dies. These are payable to the family directly and are based on the person's love, affection, services, and support. The purpose of wrongful death damages is to compensate the deceased's family for their loss of care, maintenance, support, services, advice, and counsel the deceased person would have otherwise been able to provide for them. The amount that family members can recover depends on the facts of the case, but generally they can recover for support and other financial benefits they would have received had the deceased person lived. They can recover as well for loss of love, comfort, nurturing, and companionship. Family members may also be able to recover for a reasonable amount of funeral expenses.

It is important to know which family members can recover damages for wrongful death of a loved one. In the event of a death of a family member, only family members closest to the deceased can recover. The law makes an objective decision on which family members are "closest" to the deceased and groups family members into four different categories, which include spouse and children, parents, siblings, and grandparents. The closer family members can recover for wrongful death damages to the exclusion of the others. This means that if someone dies, only those people in the highest-ranking category can recover wrongful death damages. If no one exists or is alive in that category, then people from the next category can make the claim. Any and all people who exist and are living in the category that is the "closest" can make a claim for wrongful death damages.

The categories of family members who can recover for wrongful death damages, in order of their priority, are as follows:

1. Surviving spouse and/or children of the deceased ("children" includes those who are adopted, legitimate, and illegitimate)
2. Surviving father and/or mother of the deceased, if the deceased left no spouse or child surviving ("parents" includes both biological and adoptive parents)
3. Surviving brothers and/or sisters of the deceased, if the deceased left no spouse, child, or parent surviving ("siblings" includes those by half blood, full blood, and by adoption)
4. Surviving grandparents of the deceased, if the deceased left no spouse, child, parent, or sibling surviving

> **FAST FACT**
> Wrongful death actions compensate surviving family members for their suffering and loss after the death of a loved one.

Neither grandchildren nor other relatives are entitled to recover damages for wrongful death, no matter how close they may have been to the deceased.

In conclusion, although no one can bring back a deceased loved one after an unthinkable tragedy, an experienced attorney can help a grieving family get back on its feet by holding the responsible party accountable through wrongful death and survival actions that seek financial security for family members who are qualified to make those claims.

CHAPTER 24
Liens and the Like

It is important to understand the role of liens, subrogation, reimbursements, setoff, and other encumbrances, and how they relate to personal injury litigation. These types of encumbrances can dramatically affect the amount of money you may receive from your personal injury award.

A *lien* is a demand for repayment that may be placed against your personal injury case. If another party has a valid lien against your personal injury claim, it means that even if you are successful in obtaining a money judgment or settlement from the other party involved in your accident, you may not receive that full amount; it depends on those liens or claims against your awarded amount. For this reason, it is important to understand who will be able to make a claim to a portion of your personal injury award, and under what circumstances this may occur.

A lien is a security right placed on personal property to satisfy a debt owed to a third person or entity. In the context of a personal injury award, the personal property in question is the money received from a personal injury claim, or at least the portion that the lienholder is asserting a right to recover. The most common type of lien in a personal injury case is a medical lien. In many cases, for example, the injured party may not have any health insurance, or his or her health insurance does not cover all medical bills. If this

> **FAST FACT**
> Third parties such as doctors, lawyers, and insurance companies can claim a portion of the money you are awarded in your personal injury settlement.

is the case, health care providers will seek to recover all of their unpaid medicals bills with a lien against the awarded amount. In other words, a personal injury award will likely be reduced by the amount owed for unpaid medical bills related to the auto accident. Although there are other types of liens that can affect the awarded amount, this type of lien is the most common.

Even if an insurance company has paid all of a person's medical bills, other entities may still have a claim to at least a portion of the personal injury award. When an insurance company or other entity pays medical expenses on behalf of an injured person, the company or entity likely has a claim to be reimbursed for the payments they made. Sometimes you will hear this referred to as subrogation. Although there are minor differences between subrogation and reimbursement, these two concepts essentially work in the same way. *Subrogation* means one person or party "stands in the shoes of another." For example, if an insurance company pays an injured person's medical expenses, that insurance company has the right to stand in the shoes of the injured person and collect the medical expenses paid from the awarded damages. The heart of this issue is that injured parties are not allowed "double recovery" for medical expenses (*i.e.*, having an insurance company and the at-fault party reimbursing them for their medical bills).

It is also important to understand that any amount recovered from the at-fault party could *setoff* or reduce the amount that can be recovered from a person's own auto insurance policy. This is another example of the injured party not being allowed to double recover. If a person is making a claim against his or her own insurance policy for damages, it will be reduced by any amount he or she was able to recover in litigation from the other party. For example, if a person's car is damaged in an auto accident, the amount recovered from a person's own auto insurance policy would be reduced by the amount he or she recovers from the at-fault party. This setoff principle usually comes into play when the at-fault party is uninsured or underinsured and is not able to cover the full cost of the auto accident damages. If this is the case in your accident, you may seek to recover the remaining cost from your own auto insurance policy, but would not be allowed recovery for whatever amount you were successful in obtaining from the at-fault party.

It is important to understand the types of issues with liens, subrogation, and setoff that you can encounter after receiving a personal injury award. Not only must you have a realistic expectation of the amount recoverable when considering these issues, it is also common for a personal injury attorney to spend as much time trying to resolve the issues of liens and subrogation as the actual underlying case. Each type of lien and subrogation has its own set of rules regarding if and when a person might be able to avoid or reduce paying the amount claimed. For example, federal law controls insurance policies that are created by and regulated under the Employee Retirement Income Security Act of 1974 (ERISA) and are dealt with very differently than other plans. An ERISA insurance plan may be entitled to priority reimbursement over the injured party, while other liens could be negotiated in favor of the injured party. It is for these reasons that it is important to understand these various rules, or to speak with an attorney who understands, in order to receive the maximum recovery possible.

> **FAST FACT**
> A lien is a demand for repayment that may be placed against your personal injury case.

LIENS

As discussed above, a lien is a security interest placed against a person's property to satisfy a debt owed to a third party. In a personal injury case, the money received from personal injury litigation is the property to which the lien holder is attempting to assert a right. Many different entities may try to get a portion of your award by establishing claims on the amount awarded in a personal injury case. Most people are surprised to learn that state and federal government, health insurance companies, and hospitals may be entitled to assert a claim against their personal injury award. It is important to understand the different types of liens that can be placed against a personal injury award and when they apply.

In general, there are two types of claims to look out for: statutory and contractual. A statutory lien is one that exists by a matter of law. There is no explicit agreement between the injured person and the lien holder, but the law states that the entity is entitled to enforce a lien against the personal injury award to collect money that is owed to it. The other type is a contractual lien, in which the two parties have signed a contract whereby the injured party has allowed the lien holder to enforce a lien against his or her property should he or she be granted any personal injury damages.

> **FAST FACT**
> The most common type of lien in a personal injury case is a medical lien.

Some types of statutory and contractual claims to look out for are the following:

- Medicare/Medicaid
- ERISA health insurance plans
- Veterans Administration

- Hospital
- Workers' Compensation
- Medical pay under auto insurance
- Health insurance
- Individual medical providers, such as doctors
- X-ray service providers
- Ambulance
- Chiropractors
- Prior attorneys

Some of these claims will come in the form of liens, and some will come in the form of a demand for reimbursement (otherwise known as subrogation) which was introduced earlier and will be further discussed later in this chapter. The important thing is to understand who may have the right to make a claim to a personal injury award.

The most common types of liens encountered in personal injury litigation fall into three main categories: 1) medical liens, 2) workers' compensation liens, and 3) government liens.

Medical Liens

Medical liens are those imposed by hospitals and other medical providers. In many cases, the injured party may not have any health insurance, or his or her health insurance does not cover all medical bills. In these cases, the hospital or any other health care provider will seek to recover all of their unpaid medical bills with a medical lien. These medical providers are entitled to a "lien for repayment" of any outstanding bills from treating someone who was injured in the auto accident. For example, if you are injured in an auto accident and treated at the hospital, the hospital will have a valid claim against your personal injury award for any unpaid portion of your medical bill from that treatment.

Some health care providers may ask injured parties to sign a lien letter ahead of time stating that they submit to a lien against their settlement to pay for services. This also creates a contractual lien between the parties. This is often done when the injured party has very little or no health insurance. It is an agreement to pay back the health care provider with funds received from any settlement or from the final judgment in court.

Workers' Compensation Liens

Although less common in auto accident cases, a personal injury claim can be subject to a workers' compensation lien. If a person was injured in a workplace or in a work-related accident, he or she may have received money from workers' compensation for the payment of medical bills or lost wages. In this case, it is important to know that a workers' compensation lien may be issued for whatever amounts were paid if that person is awarded damages in his or her personal injury litigation.

This typically occurs if the injured person is involved in an auto accident that is "within the course and scope" of his or her employment, such as a delivery driver. Thus, the person may be able to receive workers' compensation benefits for his or her injuries. If that happens, the workers' compensation fund may have a valid lien against any funds later received by the delivery driver in the form of a personal injury award.

Government Liens

Government liens can come in different forms, depending on which specific type of government program is applicable—but the general rule is that if the government paid a portion of the injured person's medical expenses, it has a right to enforce a lien from a personal injury award. These liens usually come in the form of Medicare, Medicaid, or Veterans Administration liens. Each type of program or agency has differing rights when it comes to placing a lien against a personal injury award.

For example, with Medicaid the applicant is required to assign his or her rights to payments for medical care from a third party to the government. This also means that even if a person on Medicaid chooses not to pursue a personal injury claim against the other party, the government has the power to do so on the Medicaid recipient's behalf in order to recover any government money used for medical payments. In a personal injury case, Medicaid has a statutory lien and is required to be reimbursed from the proceeds of the case for any medical bills. However, Medicaid liens only apply to Medicaid payments related to the injury. This means that Medicaid can only recover the costs for medical payments that were related to the injuries from the accident.

> **FAST FACT**
> Your attorney could spend as much time resolving lien and subrogation issues as he or she spends on the actual underlying case.

SUBROGATION

Subrogation is similar to a lien, and in many ways it works the same way—but it is important to understand when subrogation can apply. Although there are small legal distinctions between subrogation and reimbursement, these two things are more similar than different. Subrogation means that one person or party "stands in the shoes of another." It usually occurs when some entity, such as an insurance company, has paid expenses on behalf of an injured person, and is likely entitled to reimbursement from a third party.

Usually an insurance company will pay for the costs of treating injuries, but will contact the insured person to discuss how the injuries occurred. Among other things, the insurer is trying to determine if a third party other than the injured person could be fully or partially responsible for the injuries. This is often the case in an auto accident. The insurer will probably try to determine if the injured person is planning on suing a third party for any injuries sustained. If the personal injury litigation is successful, the insurance company will likely be owed reimbursement for any amounts awarded for costs the company previously paid.

> **FAST FACT**
> Injured parties cannot "double recover" for medical costs from both the at-fault party and their own insurance company.

Understanding all the issues with subrogation can be difficult. It is critical to be aware of potential issues (or have an attorney who is aware of them) and to be able to negotiate with the claimants. It is essential to not only fight hard with the third party to receive the injury award you deserve, but also to fight against any parties making a claim against that award to ensure they are not receiving more than they deserve.

ERISA PLANS

One type of insurance plan that it is particularly important to know more about is any plan regulated under the Employee Retirement Income Security Act of 1974, or ERISA. These are dealt with very differently than other plans. An ERISA insurance plan may be entitled to priority reimbursement over the injured party, whereas other liens may be able to be negotiated in favor of the injured party. For this reason, it is important to understand what types of health insurance plans are regulated by ERISA, as well as the laws that govern them.

ERISA governs most employee health plans and, as mentioned, many ERISA plans are under no obligation to reduce their lien. As opposed to other insurance plans, which may be required to negotiate based on the size of the personal injury award, ERISA plans argue—regardless of the circumstances of the case—that they are entitled to the entire reimbursement claim. This is not good for the injured party, who could end up with very little left of a personal injury award, depending on the size of the awarded amount.

These plans aggressively pursue reimbursement of their claim's "first dollar priority" basis with little consideration of the impact it has on the injured party. This also means that if there are several liens against the personal injury award but not enough in the award to satisfy all claims, ERISA plans will still seek to be paid in full, at a higher priority than other parties, as opposed to negotiating to ensure all parties are able to at least partially recover.

> **FAST FACT**
> Unlike other types of liens and reimbursements, ERISA plans usually cannot be negotiated and must be paid in full from the personal injury award.

There is a lot of complicated law that governs these types of insurance plans and the exact amount they are able to receive, but it is important to know that if your health insurance plan is regulated by ERISA, these types of liens can be very difficult to negotiate if they have a valid claim against a personal injury award. Therefore, it is important for the injured party to have a good understanding of what to expect prior to entering litigation or finalizing settlement.

SETOFF

The principle of setoff is also similar to reimbursement, but is applied in different situations. Many different things can offset the amount a person would be able to receive from his or her own policy. Setoff often occurs when the at-fault party is underinsured and not able to cover the full cost of the auto accident. When this is the case, the injured person would likely make a claim with his or her own auto insurance policy, but would not be allowed recovery for whatever amount he or she was successful in obtaining from the at-fault party. The total amount of recovery would be offset by what the injured person had already received.

Setoff is another way to prevent "double recovery" on the part of the injured person. This policy exists because the idea behind damages is to make the injured person "whole"—not to punish the at-fault party or provide a windfall to the injured person. For example, if the damage to your vehicle was $20,000 and the at-fault party's insurance only paid $15,000 in damages, you would probably make a claim with your own auto policy for the remaining amount, but the total amount you could receive would be offset by the $15,000 already obtained from the opposing person's insurance. Otherwise, it would result in an undeserved windfall to the injured person, which is not allowed.

Although this is the most common situation where setoff occurs, it is not the only one. An insurance company may try to offset a claim by any amount that the insurance company claims that the injured person owes. The amount owed can be in the form of unpaid premiums or funds received by the injured person from other sources. One of those sources, as discussed above, is the at-fault person's insurance—but it is not the only one, especially when dealing with uninsured/underinsured claims. Sometimes insurance companies will try to setoff amounts that an injured person received from workers' compensation or Social Security, as well as from settlements with other insurance companies.

For example, if a delivery driver was injured in an accident while working and was not at fault for the accident, the insurance company could try to offset the amount owed to the injured delivery driver by whatever amount he or she received from workers' compensation. Even if the injured delivery driver was not able to recover sufficient funds from the at-fault party, the amount recovered from his or her own insurance could be offset by any other money he or she received that was related to the accident. In this example, if the delivery driver was receiving workers' compensation benefits due to the accident, his or her claim could be offset by that amount as well as anything recovered from the at-fault party. It is important to have a good understanding of what recovery you can expect from your own insurance company, and anything that may offset that recovery.

NEGOTIATING LIENS, REIMBURSEMENTS, AND SETOFFS

Often, your lawyer can put more money in your pocket by negotiating liens, subrogation, etc. Sometimes a personal injury attorney can spend as much time, if not more, trying to resolve the issues of liens and subrogation than on the actual underlying case. Although entities may have a claim to a portion of a person's personal injury award, an experienced attorney may be able to work with those entities and negotiate a more favorable amount for the injured person.

For example, consider the all-too-common situation where an accident causes serious injuries with medical costs nearly as high as the available automobile liability insurance policy limits. If your hospital lien is $12,000 and the auto insurance coverage is limited to $15,000 (the minimal and most common coverage amount), you will not pocket much money at all. Even worse, imagine if your medical bills exceed the available insurance coverage! In these situations, it is essential to negotiate a reduction of your liens.

The main issue with these claims involves which part of a personal injury award, and how much of it, must be used to repay the claimants for money they paid or are otherwise owed. For example, it may not be clear as to what amounts are awarded for medical expenses versus other types of damages. As previously mentioned, the entity making the claim should not have greater rights than the injured person, so if the injured person was not awarded full medical expenses, an insurance company should not be entitled to full reimbursement. However, the amount that should be reimbursed is not always easy to determine. These amounts must therefore be negotiated or otherwise determined by the parties involved. This can end up being a time-consuming, drawn-out process.

The two other main theories that are used in negotiating these types of claims are the *common fund doctrine* and the *made whole doctrine*. The *common fund doctrine* is based on the idea that each entity recovering should share in the costs of seeking the recovery (*i.e.* the costs of attorneys' fees and expenses). The idea is that the claim should be reduced by some amount so that each entity making a claim to the personal injury award is paying a share of the attorneys' fees and expenses that were incurred as part of recovering the personal injury award from the third party. The *made whole doctrine*, on the other hand, is the idea that the claimant should not be reimbursed at all until the injured person is "made whole." This means that the injured person should be able to fully recover for all of his or her expenses before any other claimants are granted funds toward their liens or reimbursements. The effectiveness of these theories in negotiating depends on the type of claim and the specific law that governs it; but, as stated before, the exact amount that applies can be hard to determine.

The most important step in this process is to notify your lawyer of any potential claims an entity may have against your personal injury award. The law can be complicated, but an experienced attorney who understands the applicable law may be able to find ways to reduce, or sometimes even eliminate, a lien or reimbursement. It is critical to negotiate claims before finalizing a settlement with the third party, because the settlement will be negotiated based on how many liens, and what types of liens, exist on an award. Once the settlement is finalized, an attorney will not be able to negotiate for additional funds or reductions even if another claim on the award comes forward. For this reason, it is imperative that an attorney be aware of any potential claims up front. Keep in mind that some claims, such as ERISA claims, are very difficult to negotiate or reduce, but a well-informed and experienced attorney will have the best chance at getting the most favorable award negotiated for his or her clients.

> **FAST FACT**
> An attorney who understands the applicable laws can often negotiate many liens and reimbursements to put more money in your pocket.

CHAPTER 25
Intentional Torts

When talking about auto accident personal injury cases, we are usually referring to situations which are just that: accidents. By that we mean that the act or actions that caused the injuries were not intentional, but rather the result of some neglect, malfeasance, or mistake, which in the law is called *negligence*. It is rare to encounter an automobile "accident" that was the result of a person's deliberate or intentional action, but it is important to understand how this can affect the outcome of your auto accident personal injury case, if this were the situation. Also, these types of personal injury cases do occur more frequently when not involving auto accidents, so it is important to understand the law and rules that surround them.

> **FAST FACT**
> Intentional torts are committed on purpose, as opposed to by accident or through carelessness.

There are two main types of personal injury cases: ones that are caused by negligence and ones caused by an intentional act. The difference between accidents caused by negligence and an intentional tort is the difference between a careless act and an affirmative act. For example, if a car accident was caused by a driver failing to stop at a red light, failing to look before changing lanes, or speeding, then it likely would be determined that the accident was caused by the driver's negligence. If, on the other hand, the accident was caused by road rage, or anger on the part of the other driver, this could be considered an intentional act. If this were the case, the law of intentional torts would govern the accident, which would influence how the case was resolved. There are two areas of law that one must further understand to answer the question of negligence versus intentional acts:

1. When is an act considered an intentional tort?
2. How do intentional torts affect the outcome of an auto accident personal injury case?

DEFINING INTENTIONAL TORTS

As discussed above, intentional torts are legal wrongs that are committed on purpose, as opposed to by accident or through carelessness. The basic theory of liability states that every act of a person that causes damage to another obligates the person who was at fault to repair it. The two main theories of liability are *intentional torts* and *negligence*. An intentional tort occurs when a person acts with the intent to cause actual harm or offense to another person. Most auto accident personal injury cases, however, arise as a result of negligence, which is defined as failure to exercise reasonable care that a prudent person would exercise in a similar situation. Some examples of this are if a car accident was caused by a driver failing to stop at a red light or failing to look before changing lanes. An intentional tort, on the other hand, occurs when a person either desires to bring about a personal injury or is substantially certain that a personal injury will occur as a result of his or her actions.

In auto accident cases, the most common type of intentional tort would involve someone who caused an accident due to road rage.

> **FAST FACT**
> If an auto accident was intentionally caused by one of the parties involved, that fact can have a big outcome on the legal case against that party.

There are many ways an intentional tort can be carried out, but in this case it is one in which a motor vehicle was used as the method of causing harm. There are several types of torts, however, that fall under the category of intentional torts.

The following are some of the types of intentional torts which may or may not arise from an auto accident.

- **Battery**: Any intentional contact that is harmful or offensive constitutes battery. This applies to almost any form of harmful contact, even when no actual injury occurs.
- **Assault**: A person intentionally creates reasonable apprehension that a battery is imminent and likely to occur (*e.g.*, pointing a loaded gun at someone).
- **False Imprisonment**: A person intentionally restrains the movement of another person without the legal right to do so.
- **Intentional Infliction of Emotional Distress**: A person engages in intentional extreme or outrageous behavior that causes severe emotional distress of another.
- **Trespass to Land**: A person commits unlawful entry onto someone else's immovable property.
- **Trespass to Chattel or Conversion**: A person engages in unlawful use of or causes damage to another person's movable property (*i.e.*, car).

Notice in the above list that battery and assault are separate torts. It is possible that these torts can occur together, wherein the injured person is reasonably apprehensive of an imminent contact, and the contact then occurs. For example, if one person points a gun at another, there is probably an assault. If that person then pulls the trigger and the bullet hits the other person, there is a battery as well. However, these two types of torts do not have to occur together. For example, if the person never fires the gun, there is assault without battery. Conversely, if the person shoots the other in the back, there may be battery without assault, because the person being shot never knew the threat of harmful contact existed before it occurred.

You can see how this concept can be applied to an auto accident case. Generally, if there were an intentional tort car accident case, we would be looking specifically at the intentional tort of battery, but you can imagine how there could be an assault tort involved as well. If a person uses his or her vehicle to intentionally cause harm to another person by causing an accident, this would be considered an intentional battery. If the person also threatened to hit the injured person with his or her car, and the injured person saw him or her coming from a distance at high speed, there could be an assault tort as well. If, on the other hand, the person intended to cause the accident, but the injured person had no knowledge it was about to occur, there would likely only be a battery without assault tort. In auto accident cases, these are the two types of intentional torts that will usually be applicable, so it is important to know more about what constitutes each of these types of torts.

> **FAST FACT**
> If a person caused an accident on purpose, whether due to road rage or some other circumstance, it would likely be considered an intentional tort.

Battery

Battery is an intentional contact that is harmful or offensive resulting from an act intended to cause the person to receive that contact. In other words, it is the harmful or offensive contact of a person, when another person meant for that contact to occur. In the case of an auto accident, the harmful or offensive contact in question can occur through the use of a personal vehicle.

There are essentially three elements that must be present for the intentional tort of battery to exist:

1. Intent to commit the act,
2. Contact with another person, and
3. Harm or offense

Intent signifies that the person committing the tort was substantially certain that the act would cause contact that is harmful or offensive. This means that battery could be committed without the intent to inflict actual damage. It is enough that the person intended to inflict harmful or offensive contact without the other person's consent. In other a words, if a person did not intend to cause damage but intended the contact, then that represents sufficient intent for the purpose of committing a battery. The person could also have either desired the physical damage result from the act, or known that it was likely to occur.

Contact is the touching of another's person, or of something closely connected to the person. In the case of a car accident, there is little doubt that contact would have occurred, but this goes to show that any amount of contact to a person or something connected to a person (*i.e.*, a car) is sufficient contact to constitute a battery. The upshot is that there is no minimum amount of contact that needs to be established to show a battery occurred, as long as the other elements are present.

The final element is that a **Harm** or **Offense** occurred. Damage is not necessarily required, but in the case of an auto accident it would be all but necessary in order for you to have any recovery. This is because there are other types of battery that exist where "damage" would not be required. This would be true, for example, if someone were to spit in another's face. Although the contact may not have caused damage, it would still be considered harmful or offensive. In the case of an auto accident, the harmful contact would be considered the damage to one's vehicle and the injury to one's person. It would be unlikely in that event to have any recovery without actual damage or injury. To reiterate, however, there is no minimum amount of damage one needs to show to establish that a battery occurred.

Assault

Although not always as common, another type of intentional tort that may arise from an auto accident is assault. Assault is different from battery, in that an assault is the imminent threat that a battery will occur. If battery is the intentional harmful or offensive contact of another person, an assault is the threat that contact will occur—whether it does or not. Again, the difference between assault and battery and negligence is that assault and battery are both intentional, whereas negligence is unintentional.

The three elements that must be present to determine that an assault has occurred are:

1. Reasonable apprehension of an imminent battery,
2. Intent to commit the act, and
3. Apparent ability or means to carry out the threat.

The main element of assault is the **reasonable apprehension** of imminent battery. That means a person perceives that a battery is about to be committed upon him or her. One does not necessarily need be "afraid" of the act that is about to happen, but one's apprehension must be both reasonable and imminent. That means, for example, if someone verbally threatens to run another person over with his or her car, but the person is in the middle of an airport, this may not constitute an assault because it is not reasonable to believe the person who made the threat could carry it out—and even if it were reasonable, the threat is not imminent. If, on the other hand, the person was sitting in a vehicle which was pointed at the other person, and started driving towards him or her, this would likely constitute an assault (even without a verbal threat) so long as the injured person saw that it was about to happen. This is because the injured person would have a reasonable and imminent apprehension of being hit by a car.

The second element, as with battery and all other intentional torts, is that the person committing the act had the **intention** to do so. In the case of an assault, the person does not have to have the intent to actually go through with the act (*e.g.,* hitting another person with a car), but merely the intent to cause the other to believe that it would be done. This means that the person does not have to have the intent to hit someone with his or her car, just the intent to threaten to do so. If this person caused someone apprehension of receiving a battery by accidentally veering off the road, however, this would not constitute an assault on the person.

To constitute an assault, there must not just be a threat of battery, but the **ability** to carry out those threats. The law deems that one has the ability to carry out threats when the person appears to have the means to complete the battery. If we go back to the example in the airport, a person threatening to run another over another person with a car in an airport does not have the apparent means to complete that act. If he is sitting in his car at the time he makes that statement, and the other person in standing on the sidewalk, then that would constitute having the means to carry out his threat.

HOW INTENTIONAL TORTS AFFECT THE OUTCOME OF A CASE

Insurance companies will treat car accidents caused by intentional torts differently than accidents caused by negligence. Many auto insurance policies do not cover intentional torts. Although they do cover the vast majority of accidents, which are caused by negligence, intentional torts such as battery and assault fall under the policies' exclusions. As a result, a different legal strategy will need to be developed in order to recover for the accident.

Insurance companies do not cover intentional torts because then their clients could commit crimes, such as battery and assault, and have their insurance companies pay for the damage they intentionally caused. As a public policy matter, this would offer an unhealthy advantage to those who intentionally cause damage to others. It is beneficial to society as a whole to deter people from committing intentional torts by not covering the damages they cause, but this can often leave those injured in the lurch with no real party from which to recover. For this reason, it is not always advantageous to bring a case against a person who has committed an intentional tort. Although it seems unfair, since their insurance company will likely not cover the damage, there is not a high likelihood of success if the person does not have the resources to pay for the damage he or she caused. This is why it is important to be able to argue that the person's actions were of negligence rather than an intentional act, if possible.

Insurance companies will also try to use the argument that an accident was caused intentionally just to avoid paying damages. It may seem somewhat counterintuitive, but since intentional accidents often preclude insurance companies from being liable for paying any damages, it is in their interest to attempt the argument that their client purposefully caused the accident when the situation warrants it. It is important to know the facts of the case and the surrounding law to determine if that assertion is valid. The injured person needs to be able to argue that the accident was caused by negligence, if possible. If the accident was, in fact, caused by intentional tort, it may still be possible for a person to recover from his or her own insurance company. For these reasons, it is important to understand the law that surrounds intentional torts. No matter what, intentional tort cases can be some of the most difficult cases to pursue.

> **FAST FACT**
> Most insurance policies do not cover intentional torts.

PART III:
MEDICAL MATTERS

CHAPTER 26
Common Traumatic Injuries

Motor vehicle accidents can cause a wide variety of traumatic injuries. The possibilities are endless, from minor muscle aches to loss of limb. However, spine injuries in the back and neck are by far the most common cause of accident-related pain and suffering. These problems, and a few other common traumatic injuries, are discussed in more detail below.

At times, it is difficult to pinpoint exactly where, anatomically, you are injured or what, diagnostically, is wrong. Some injuries result in a delayed impact. They cause pain long after the accident. The anatomical source of the pain is not always clear. Nevertheless, determining the type of injury caused by the accident is essential to your case. The nature of your injury has a major impact on the value of your claims. For example, in general, spinal injuries are worth more than arm, leg, or shoulder problems. Brain injuries are usually more valuable than neck and back injuries. Permanent nerve damage injuries, like herniated discs in the spine, typically bring larger settlements or judgments than broken bones that will eventually heal (even a fractured spine!) or soft-tissue muscular injuries. Injuries leading to surgery are worth far more than non-surgical harm.

> **FAST FACT**
> Spine injuries causing neck pain and lower back pain are commonplace in car accident cases.

SPINAL INJURIES

Spine problems are commonplace in automobile accidents. They occur most frequently in the lower back, also known as the lumbar spine, and the neck, called the cervical spine. Less often, accident-related spine pain arises in middle back (thoracic spine) or the tailbone (sacral spine).

Traumatic injury symptoms typically originate from the following anatomic structures in and around the spine:

- Muscles
- Nerves
- Discs
- Joints
- Bones

It is often difficult to diagnose the exact location of the pain source because symptoms arising from different spinal tissues can feel extremely similar. Therefore, it is a challenge to differentiate the potential pain sources without using interventional diagnostic procedures. The problem that uncertain pain source diagnosis presents for injured accident victims is that the confusion clouds the issue of whether the accident or a preexisting condition caused their injuries. Determining the type of spine tissue causing your pain could help you prove your case against the other driver's insurance company.

> **FAST FACT**
> You need your doctor to diagnose the specific spinal tissue causing your pain, because it matters greatly in determining the value of your claims.

Spine pain can be constant or intermittent. It can be acute (lasting 12 weeks or less) or chronic (remaining more than 12 weeks).

Sometimes it presents as a dull ache. Other times it is sharp, piercing, or burning. Neck and back symptoms can be radicular in nature, meaning that nerve roots are affected and the pain may radiate into arms, legs, hands, and feet. It is often accompanied by numbness, tingling, and weakness. Spine pain can cause trouble sleeping, concentrating, and other major problems with daily living.

Below is a brief summary of common back injuries that result from motor vehicle accidents.

Back Pain

Low back pain, called lumbago by doctors, is both common and disabling. Indeed, back pain is the leading cause of disability worldwide. It is estimated that low back problems cause approximately 40% of all missed work days. Lumbago is a top five reason for visits to the doctor. Most adults experience some level of back pain during their lifetime. However, back pain caused by car accident trauma generally proves far more painful and debilitating than the usual wear-and-tear back symptoms.

Back pain has numerous potential causes. Determining the source of your symptoms is important to your personal injury case. If possible, you need your doctor to diagnose the specific spinal tissue causing the pain. Whether the problem arises from the muscles, bones, intervertebral discs, nerves, or joints matters greatly in determining the value of your claims. Sometimes this can be determined without diagnostic imaging, but typically the use of diagnostics such as magnetic resonance imaging (MRI) is helpful, and perhaps necessary.

Neck Pain

Neck injuries, like back injuries, commonly arise out of automobile accidents. "Whiplash" is a non-medical term used to describe a common neck injury that occurs in automobile accidents. Technically, whiplash is usually a cervical strain, which means that the muscles and tendons that support the neck are injured. When you are in an automobile accident, the force that is swiftly exerted upon your neck often causes whiplash. If you experience whiplash, you may also be experiencing neck sprain as opposed to neck strain. Neck injury symptoms include neck pain, stiffness, tightness, limited range of motion, headaches, dizziness, arm pain, and shoulder pain.

Disc Injuries

Between each of the bones in your back, there is a soft inner disc, the nucleus pulposus, which is surrounded by a harder outer wall, the annulus fibrosus. These flexible, rubbery, jelly donut-shaped discs essentially act as cushions between your back bones, called vertebrae. Intervertebral discs do not show up on x-rays the way bones do. Therefore, disc injuries are rarely diagnosed without the benefit of an MRI or other advanced imaging diagnostic device. Unfortunately, cervical and lumbar spinal disc injuries do not heal like soft-tissue injuries such as muscle strains and sprains. They are typically permanent in nature, and they gradually worsen over time.

> **FAST FACT**
> Disc injuries are rarely diagnosed without the benefit of an MRI or other advanced imaging diagnostic device.

Sometimes, the hard outer ring tears and the soft material inside of each disc leaks or is pushed out, causing severe pain by affecting the surrounding nerves. When this happens, it is known as a herniated, ruptured, prolapsed, or slipped disc. (The use of the term "slipped disc" is not medically accurate because the spinal discs are firmly attached between the vertebrae and cannot "slip"). Often, herniated lumbar discs cause spinal stenosis, a condition where the spinal canal narrows and compresses the spinal cord or surrounding nerves.

A similar but less severe injury called a bulging disc or protrusion occurs when the outermost layers of the anulus fibrosus are still intact, but they bulge when the disc is under pressure, causing severe pain. In some instances, disc injuries can cause pain by releasing inflammatory chemicals even in the absence of nerve root compromise.

Disc injuries can be caused by trauma, such as a car accident, or age-related wear and tear called degenerative disc disease. Disc injury symptoms vary depending on the location and severity of the herniation, bulge, or irritation. In some instances, disc injuries can be asymptomatic, or pain free, for years. Indeed, many people do not even know they suffer from undiagnosed disc disease. Other, less fortunate disc injury sufferers experience severe and unrelenting pain that radiates into the arms, legs, hands, and feet. Additional symptoms could include sensory changes like numbness, tingling, muscular weakness, paralysis, and impaired reflexes. Irritation of the nerves surrounding the spine is also common in disc injuries. Intervertebral disc problems are often associated with "pinched nerves" in the neck and back.

> **FAST FACT**
> Radiculopathy, commonly known as a "pinched nerve" or nerve root impingement, is a condition where one or more nerves are not working properly.

Because disc injuries do not heal like muscular injuries, sometimes surgery is required to treat the problem. However, in the majority of cases, spine surgery is not required. Initial treatment usually consists of conservative methods such as non-narcotic pain medications, exercises, physical therapy, and/or chiropractic treatment. If pain persists, injections are considered, such as epidural steroid injections, facet blocks, trigger point injections, etc. Next, minimally invasive surgeries such as radiofrequency ablation, or rhizotomy, are offered as a treatment option. Traditional invasive back surgeries such as discectomy, partial removal of the injured disc, or spinal fusion, a surgery that joins two or more vertebrae, are a last resort.

Radiculopathy

Radiculopathy, commonly known as a "pinched nerve," is a condition where one or more nerves are not working properly. It involves neuropathy, damage affecting nerves that may impair sensation, movement, and other aspects of health. It is caused by a mechanical compression or inflammation of a nerve root. With cervical and lumbar radiculopathy, the location of the injury is at or near the root of nerves in the neck or back, near the junction of the root and the spinal cord. However, spine pain and symptoms radiate to other parts of the body served by the affected nerves, such as the arms, legs, shoulders, fingers, or toes. Radiculopathy is often called "nerve root impingement".

> **FAST FACT**
> Spine pain and symptoms radiate to other parts of the body served by the affected nerves, such as the arms, legs, shoulders, fingers, or toes.

To diagnose radiculopathy, doctors perform several specialized tests, such as the straight leg test, during physical examination.

They also rely on diagnostics such as MRI, EMG (Electromyography), and NCS (Nerve Conduction Study).

Vertebral Fracture

A fracture is a medical condition involving a break in the continuity of a bone. A fractured vertebra occurs whenever compression on the spine causes a bone to essentially break and collapse. Spinal fractures can cause severe pain that is intensified by standing or walking. Obviously, a broken back or neck is an extremely serious injury that can result in death or paralysis if the spinal cord is involved. Fortunately, such devastating injuries are extraordinarily uncommon in the context of auto accidents.

Doctors treat vertebral compression fractures with conservative methods such as medication and orthopedic braces. They also treat broken necks and backs surgically with kyphoplasty and vertebroplasty procedures. While vertebral fractures can certainly be severe and debilitating, in many cases they heal faster and more completely than intervertebral disc injuries.

Sprain and Strain

A series of muscles, tendons, and ligaments in your back hold the bones in your spinal column in place. Insurance adjusters and personal injury lawyers call this portion of your anatomy "soft tissues" to distinguish them from the surrounding vertebrae and intervertebral discs. Doctors cannot objectively verify soft-tissue injuries using diagnostic testing like MRI and x-ray the way they can with herniated discs and broken bones. Instead, sprains and strains are diagnosed based solely on medical history and physical examination.

> **FAST FACT**
> Unlike spinal disc injuries, sprains and strains usually heal fairly quickly. Most soft-tissue injuries are resolved within a few months.

While spinal strains and sprains are technically two different kinds of injuries, many of the symptoms are similar. Back or neck strain, also known as a "pulled muscle," occurs when the muscles or tendons that support the spine are injured. More specifically, a spine strain results from the muscles stretching too far, causing tiny tears of the tissue and weakening the muscles to the point that they are not able to hold the bones of the spinal column in place correctly. This causes the spine to become less stable, resulting in back pain, stiffness, limited mobility, and muscle spasms.

On the other hand, a back or neck sprain occurs when a ligament is injured by a stretch or a tear. Ligaments are the body parts that connect one bone to another and prevent excessive movement of the joint. Like a strain, a sprain causes instability in the spinal column that results in back or neck pain, stiffness, limited mobility, and muscle spasms.

Unlike disc injuries, sprains and strains usually heal fairly quickly. Most soft-tissue injuries are resolved within a few months. Of course, everyone heals at his or her own pace, and some injuries last longer. Typical treatments for spine strains and sprains include rest, ice packs, heat therapy, pain medication, anti-inflammatory medication, muscle relaxants, massage therapy, physical therapy, and chiropractic treatment.

BRAIN INJURIES

Traumatic brain injuries (TBI), also known as intracranial injuries, are head injuries that can vary in severity from a mild concussion to severe brain damage. When the brain is jarred or shaken in a car wreck, the impact can cause bruising, swelling, or tearing of the brain tissue. TBI symptoms include unconsciousness, headaches, dizziness, sadness, anger, confusion, trouble concentrating, memory loss, nausea, vomiting, fatigue, drowsiness, and seizures. These problems can be temporary or permanent.

Doctors use a variety of methods to diagnose head injuries. They will begin by taking your medical history, asking questions designed to test your ability to pay attention, learn, remember, and solve problems. They will also physically examine you for physical indicators of TBI by checking your strength, balance, reflexes, coordination, and sensation. Finally, they may order advanced diagnostics such as MRI or CT scan testing.

Brain injury cases can involve serious damages and result in large monetary awards. However, they are extraordinarily difficult to diagnose and prove. Think about it: If you are suffering from memory loss and confusion symptoms, will you be able to tell your doctor about these problems? Considering the challenges inherent to TBI diagnosis, if you or someone who cares about you notices any head injury symptoms following an accident, please bring a loved one who knows you well with you to the doctor. Often a spouse, parent, or significant other will be able to report changes and symptoms you cannot notice or remember.

Doctors treat TBI with a variety of options, including medicine; physical, occupational, and speech therapy; counseling; support groups; and even brain surgery.

FACIAL INJURIES

Motor vehicle accidents sometimes cause bruises, breaks, or cuts to the face. Indeed, you might break your nose, your jaw, your cheekbone or other bones. Swelling, bruising, pain, visible deformity, and bleeding in the area impacted could all be signs of a bone fracture or a broken bone. In the case of a broken nose, symptoms include swollen nose, tenderness, bruising around the eyes, nose bleed, audible noise when the nose is touched, and difficulty breathing through the nose. Cheekbone fracture results in asymmetry of your cheekbones, altered sensations on your face or particularly below the eye on the side of your potential injury, jaw pain, blood on the side of the eye, and vision problems such as blurriness. Dislocation or fracture of the jaw causes bruising or swelling on your jaw or near your ear, a feeling your teeth are misaligned, teeth actually missing, difficulty opening your mouth, and jaw pain in general. If you have an eye socket fracture, you may notice a visibly sunken eye, pain when moving the eye, numbness of the eye, double vision, or altered feeling beneath the eye that was injured. Finally, if the windshield or windows break as a result of the collision, severe lacerations and permanent facial scarring from broken glass are possible.

In additional to the traditional medical attention necessary to heal your facial injuries, you should consider whether cosmetic surgery is necessary. If it is, the other driver's insurance company could be liable to cover these damages as well.

OTHER PHYSICAL INJURIES

Aside from the above mentioned injuries, you should keep a look out for other injuries that you may have experienced in your automobile accident. Other common injuries that you should look for when you are involved in an automobile accident include shoulder injuries, leg injuries, knee injuries, foot injuries, chest injuries, and abdominal injuries. These are generally characterized by pain in the area where your injury is located. Inability to use the body part or experiencing pain when using the particular body part you may have injured can be an indicator of injury as well. When you feel pain or a part of your body simply does not feel right after an automobile accident, it is better to check out the issue than to ignore it.

CHAPTER 27
Health Care Treatment Options

As mentioned previously, it is absolutely essential to your case that you verify your injuries by seeking medical attention from a licensed doctor as soon as possible after the accident.

To that end, you have numerous health care provider options:

- Emergency room
- Family practice
- Urgent care
- After-hours clinic
- Neurology
- Orthopedics
- Pain management
- Rheumatology
- Radiology
- Chiropractic
- Physical therapy
- Occupational therapy
- Mental health care
- Other licensed health care providers

Once you have selected a doctor for treatment, given your physician a complete and accurate medical history (including all accident-related symptoms), and submitted yourself for physical examination and diagnostic testing, you must follow your doctor's treatment

FAST FACT

Follow your doctor's treatment advice and go to every scheduled medical appointment.

advice and go to every scheduled medical appointment. With so many qualified health care options, choosing a doctor can be difficult. Therefore, it may help to break the decision down step-by-step.

First, you must decide whether to go to the emergency room (ER) immediately after the accident. If you begin experiencing pain at the scene of the accident, especially severe pain, a trip to the ER is probably a good idea. If your pain is extreme or you are disoriented or confused, you should consider allowing an ambulance to transport you. The ER can check your vitals and take x-rays to rule out broken bones. However, in most instances the ER will not order an MRI, so they will be unable to determine whether you have a disc injury in your neck or back. Usually, at the time of discharge the ER will provide instructions to follow up with your primary care physician and other specialists as required. The upside of the ER is that it is a great precautionary measure to treat or rule out urgent acute injuries; the downside is that ER bills are extraordinarily expensive.

> **FAST FACT**
> If you forgo the ER and you have a primary care or family physician, that is often the best doctor to see first.

If you elect to forgo the ER, you should nevertheless see a doctor as soon as any pain or other symptoms arise. If you have a primary care or family doctor, that is typically the best place to start, assuming you can schedule a prompt appointment. Another decent starting point would be an urgent care center or an after-hours clinic.

Whether you began your medical treatment at the ER, family doctor, or after-hours clinic, you should consider seeing a specialist if your symptoms persist more than a few weeks after the accident.

Below is a basic description of some, but not all, of your options. As you will see, there are many paths to healing traumatic injuries arising out of car, truck, and motorcycle accidents.

It might be a good idea to discuss these options with your personal injury attorney before scheduling your appointment. You will find that not all doctors—or even every excellent physician—are interested in treating patients injured in automobile accidents. Some doctors decline patients who face potential litigation because they have no interest in reporting, corresponding, or testifying to attorneys. It is essential to your case that the doctor you choose is not only able to treat you competently, but is also capable and willing to communicate your injuries' diagnosis, causation, prognosis, and costs to the attorneys involved in your case. Your doctor is just as important to proving your injuries as he or she is to healing your wounds.

> **FAST FACT**
> Consider seeing a specialist if your symptoms persist for more than a few weeks after the accident.

EMERGENCY MEDICINE

Emergency medicine is a specialty involving care for patients with acute injuries and illnesses that require immediate medical attention. Treatment in the ER generally involves medical conditions that need immediate care that are particularly severe or acute in nature. Health care providers in this realm of medicine provide care for most traumatic injuries. However, emergency medicine is not an option for long-term, rehabilitative care. Aptly named, you should generally only seek the help of emergency medicine providers in the case of an emergency situation where care cannot or should not be delayed—an emergency!

Discussed above is the decision of whether to visit the ER after a motor vehicle accident. Of course, you should also understand that sometimes after an automobile accident, emergency responders will bring you to the ER whether you request it or not. One example is if you are unconscious. Another would be if you are otherwise incapacitated.

Whether you visit the ER of your own volition or while unconscious, the important takeaway is that the ER should not be your last medical visit. You should follow up with your family doctor or a specialist to treat or rule out long-term injuries.

FAMILY MEDICINE

Visiting a general practitioner, particularly your family physician or internist, after an automobile accident is an excellent place to start. This is the doctor who likely knows you best. He or she will have records that can reflect changes in your condition before and after the automobile accident. From there, your doctor can help you pinpoint what injuries may have resulted from the accident. General practitioners have a broad range of knowledge of many different kinds of medicine, and this allows them to refer you to other specialists who can further help you treat your conditions. Frequently, you will not visit your general practitioner about the injury after he or she refers you to another health care provider who specializes in treating your injury.

Though they may not be able to treat your condition, visiting your general practitioner after an accident is wise. He or she will be able to analyze your symptoms and send you in the right direction for additional care.

If you do not already have a family doctor or internist, consider visiting an urgent care center or after-hours clinic. They can provide many of the services a primary care physician would offer.

NEUROLOGY

Neurology is a branch of medicine that specializes in disorders of the nervous system. This means that neurologists and neurosurgeons are doctors who work with patients who suffer from spine and brain injuries. Therefore, if you were involved in an automobile accident that caused trauma to your back, neck, or head, a doctor specializing in neurology may be able to help you.

Though neurologists and neurosurgeons practice in similar realms, they are technically two distinct types of doctors. A neurologist typically focuses on the investigation, diagnosis, treatment, and therapy of neurological injuries and illnesses. Neurologists manage conditions for patients non-surgically and they counsel patients through the appropriate treatments. Neurosurgeons are essentially neurologists' corresponding surgical specialists. Therefore, in addition to diagnosing neurological injuries, neurosurgeons decide what surgical options are appropriate for the patient and perform both traditionally invasive and minimally invasive surgeries to improve the conditions.

Neurologists and neurosurgeons are uniquely qualified to treat TBI, headaches, and other head injuries. Like many of the other types of doctors listed below, neurological specialists are also adept at treating spinal disc injuries and spinal fractures.

ORTHOPEDICS

Orthopedic specialists focus on the musculoskeletal system, so they treat numerous common traumatic injuries caused by car accidents. Like neurosurgeons, orthopedic surgeons are qualified to perform back and neck surgery. Indeed, orthopedic surgeons operate on a wide variety of injured body parts, such as bones, joints, discs, ligaments, tendons, and muscles. Bone fractures, dislocations, herniated spinal discs, strains, sprains, muscle injuries, tendon injuries, ligament injuries, spinal injuries, and other kinds of injuries that result from automobile accidents are treated by orthopedic surgeons. These health care providers sometimes choose to specialize in the types of injuries they treat as well as the impacted areas of the body that they treat. This means that some orthopedic surgeons focus on only the spine, while others operate on shoulders, knees, elbows, and other frequently-injured joints.

Like neurologists, orthopedic specialists are excellent at treating spine injuries. They offer both surgical and non-surgical treatment options. Although orthopedic doctors treat a wider variety of body parts than their colleagues in neurology, orthopedists do not treat head injuries such as TBI.

PAIN MANAGEMENT

Pain management is a branch of medicine employing an interdisciplinary approach for easing the suffering and improving the quality of life of patients living with pain. Pain clinics employ doctors trained in a variety of specialties, including neurology, orthopedics, anesthesiology, and physiatry. Pain specialists are experts at diagnosing the cause of pain and treating it. They focus on bone, muscle, and nerve injuries. This makes them well qualified to handle the traumatic back, neck, and head injuries so prevalent with auto accidents.

Pain management uses the latest research available to offer the newest, most effective treatments to minimize pain, as well as time-tested mainstays such as medications, physical therapy, injections, electrical stimulations, minimally invasive surgeries, and psychological support. The ultimate goal of these doctors is to find the source of your debilitating pain and rehabilitate you. If you are experiencing any kind of pain that you believe is associated with an automobile accident in which you were involved, a pain specialist may be able to help you.

RHEUMATOLOGY

Rheumatology is a sub-specialty in internal medicine dedicated to diagnosis and therapy of rheumatic diseases, a non-specific term for medical problems affecting the joints and/or connective tissue. Clinicians who specialize in rheumatology are called rheumatologists. Rheumatologists deal mainly with clinical problems involving joints, soft tissues, autoimmune diseases, vasculitis, and heritable connective tissue disorders.

Back pain and neck pain are among the few major rheumatic disorders currently recognized. Rheumatologists prove particularly effective at treating soft-tissue injuries in the cervical and lumbar spines where MRI and other diagnostic tests are unable to objectively reveal the source of the pain. In the absence of objective diagnostics like MRI images revealing herniated spinal discs, rheumatologists are often helpful in proving your pain was caused by the accident rather than a preexisting condition.

RADIOLOGY

Radiology is a medical specialty that uses imaging technology to diagnose and treat disease seen within the body. Radiologists use a variety of imaging techniques such as X-ray radiography, ultrasound, computed tomography (CT), nuclear medicine, positron emission tomography (PET), and magnetic resonance imaging (MRI) to interpret and analyze information needed to diagnose or treat diseases.

Typically, when in need of an X-ray or MRI, your treating doctor will order that diagnostic test and a radiologist will then review the images, analyze the contents, and issue a report interpreting the results. Occasionally, the radiology report will suggest additional diagnostic testing. In limited instances, radiologists can administer certain treatments to patients. However, in most instances where you seek the help of a radiologist in the context of your automobile accident injuries, that doctor will probably not treat you beyond interpreting your diagnostic imaging.

Sometimes your treating physician will rely solely on the radiologist's report, but usually your treating neurologist, orthopedist, or pain management specialist will review the actual images in addition to the radiology report.

CHIROPRACTIC

Chiropractic care provides a useful alternative to traditional medicine for treating auto accident injuries, especially back and neck problems. These specialists emphasize diagnosis, treatment, and prevention of mechanical disorders of the musculoskeletal system, especially the spine, under the belief that these disorders affect general health through the nervous system. Chiropractors focus on the conservative management of the neuromusculoskeletal system without the use of surgery or drugs, placing a special emphasis on the spine.

Back and neck pain are the specialties of chiropractic care. The focus of chiropractic practice is the vertebral subluxation or spinal joint subluxation, dysfunctional biomechanical spinal displacements that actively alter neurological function. Subluxations interfere with the body's function.

Chiropractors utilize manipulation of the musculoskeletal system, particularly the spine, called "spinal adjustment" or "chiropractic adjustment." In short, chiropractic doctors manually adjust bones of the spine in order to treat the patient. Chiropractic adjustment is a passive manual maneuver during which a three-joint complex is taken past the normal range of movement, but not so far as to dislocate or damage the joint. The process is defined by a dynamic thrust—a sudden force that causes an audible release and attempts to increase a joint's range of motion. Chiropractic diagnosis may involve a range of methods including skeletal imaging, observational and tactile assessments, and other evaluations. In many instances, especially when an MRI reveals disc injuries, a chiropractor may refer a patient to an appropriate medical doctor or specialist, or co-manage the patient with another health care provider.

Many chiropractors highlight their ability to help with whiplash, which of course frequently results from automobile accidents. They are quite capable of treating many other traumatic injuries.

PHYSICAL AND OCCUPATIONAL THERAPY

Over many years of practicing personal injury law, I have noticed an interesting trend: my severely injured clients love their physical therapists. When you consider that the hours they spend together are extremely painful and incredibly challenging, this fact is genuinely impressive. Physical therapy is one profession that has the whole "client satisfaction thing" figured out!

Physical therapy, also called physiotherapy or abbreviated as "PT", is a health care profession that remediates impairments and promotes mobility, function, and quality of life through examination, diagnosis, and physical intervention (using mechanical force and movement). The primary physical therapy practitioner is the physical therapist (also called a "PT") who is trained and licensed to examine, evaluate, diagnose and treat impairment, functional limitations, and disabilities in patients or clients. PTs are assisted by physical therapist assistants. Physical therapy must be prescribed by a doctor, meaning that you cannot directly book an appointment for physical therapy without a doctor's note.

Though physical therapy and occupational therapy share similar characteristics, such as the goal of rehabilitation, they are actually distinct treatment options. When you are involved in an automobile accident, you may experience an injury that will require therapy to ensure a full recovery. Whenever you are unable to perform physical functions that you were able to perform before your accident, you may need to see a physical or occupational therapist.

Physical therapists treat a variety of physically limiting symptoms caused by injuries. In general, they aim to relieve their patients' pain as well as treat their patients' mobility problems that relate to strength, balance, endurance, and other aspects. When you seek treatment from physical therapists, they will usually work in a hands-on fashion in order to improve your condition. Generally, physical therapists will design a treatment plan for you and help you achieve certain goals. These will often include treatments such as soft-tissue massage and balance training. A physical therapist will help you with more general goals like improving balance or regaining control over body parts.

Occupational therapists are focused on rehabilitating their patients in different realms of life such as work, leisure, and everyday life functions. An occupational therapist will generally look at the physical limitations of a patient and analyze what kind of treatment is appropriate. These treatments will often include a mixture of exercises that will help you regain the ability, control, and function you had over a particular body part before your injury. The ultimate goal of occupational therapists is narrower than those of physical therapists in the sense that they are generally focused on improving function in particular realms of life or work. For instance, they may help patients specifically with regaining functions that are vital to their individual jobs.

MENTAL HEALTH CARE

Unfortunately, auto accidents can damage you beyond the physical injuries described above. Sometimes, your mental health is diminished. The emotional and psychological consequences of a motor vehicle crash can be even tougher to take than back and neck injuries.

Mental health refers to your level of psychological well-being or the absence of a mental disorder. Good mental health means you are functioning at a satisfactory level of emotional and behavioral adjustment. According to the World Health Organization

(WHO), mental health includes "subjective well-being, perceived self-efficacy, autonomy, competence, intergenerational dependence, and self-actualization of one's intellectual and emotional potential, among others."

Mental health specialists often treat patients who have experienced situations, such as violent vehicle collisions with resulting injuries, which have left them with pain, suffering, anxiety, shock, emotional distress, or other mental health ailments. In an automobile accident, these professionals often treat the above mentioned conditions, as a car accident can spur those conditions in victims. If you believe that you are experiencing any of the above conditions, a mental health specialist may be able to help you improve your condition. Many kinds of doctors and other professionals treat mental health problems:

- Psychiatrists
- Clinical psychologists
- Clinical social workers
- Mental health counselors

If you feel as though your levels of emotional and behavioral well-being have been harmed as a result of the accident, please discuss this with your treating physician, personal injury lawyer, or someone else you trust who can assist you in scheduling an appointment with a mental health professional.

CHAPTER 28
Medical Mistakes to Avoid

When dealing with doctors, a single mistake can ruin your car accident claim.

It is essential to your personal injury case that your doctors and other health care providers report all your injuries and symptoms caused or aggravated by the motor vehicle accident. Complete and accurate doctor reports are crucial to the successful handling of your bodily injury claims. Ideally, your doctors' reports will 1) set forth all of your injuries and symptoms; 2) describe your pain and suffering; 3) relate your injuries, symptoms, and treatment to the accident; and 4) express an opinion on any related future problems, treatment, restrictions, and disability.

> **FAST FACT**
> Complete and accurate doctor reports are critical to your case.

Below is a list of eleven mistakes to avoid when dealing with your doctors after an accident injury.

1. **Failure to promptly seek medical attention after the accident.** As the plaintiff, you bear the burden of proving that the accident caused or aggravated your injury symptoms. Do not expect the insurance company, judge, or jury to believe that the accident caused your injuries if you neglect to visit a doctor shortly after the accident. Please do not ignore accident injury symptoms, even if they seem minor and you hope or expect them to heal soon. Often, accident injury symptoms—especially back and neck pain—slowly worsen after

the accident. If you wait too late to seek treatment, you may doom your case. Don't wait until it is too late!

2. **Failure to provide your doctor with a complete and accurate medical history.** In addition to discussing your current injury symptoms and the auto accident that caused them, your doctor will probably ask you about any and all injuries and illnesses suffered before your car crash. Physicians call this your "medical history." Be sure to think hard about your prior medical treatment and tell your physician everything you can recall, even if you had prior accidents or pre-existing conditions. This will help your doctor get you well, and it will help your attorney win your case. Concealing prior accidents, injuries, and medical treatment could doom your case. Just be honest and forthcoming with your doctors. If you had prior medical problems, tell your doctor and emphasize how your new, accident-related symptoms are different and worse than your prior problems.

3. **Missed medical appointments.** Like waiting too long to see the doctor, the mistake of missing appointments could be characterized as "undertreating" your injuries and it might result in the ruination of your bodily injury claims. Failure to regularly attend all scheduled medical appointments will empower the insurance company to argue that you either (a) were not hurting or (b) were not serious about getting better. Either characterization could be a case killer! Moreover, failure to show up as scheduled could irritate or mislead your doctors, the key witnesses for proving your injuries.

4. **Failure to describe your pain and symptoms.** Do not expect insurance adjusters, judges, or juries to "take your word for it" that you were in severe pain as a result of the accident. They will need your doctor to "put it in writing" by reporting

it in your medical records. Therefore, you should report all of your accident-related symptoms every time you visit the doctor. Do not shy away from repeating the same complaints every visit if your symptoms persist. Also, do not hesitate to be as specific as possible. For example, do not just tell your doctor that you are suffering from neck pain if your neck pain is specific in nature, such as burning, stabbing, or radiating pain with numbness and tingling.

5. **Failure to inform your doctor that your injury has affected your ability to work.** Your ability to work and earn a living could be a huge part of your personal injury case. If you are making a claim for loss of wages, then your doctor's opinion on your level of disability is a key factor in your case. Insurance adjusters, judges, and juries will not believe that your ability to work has been affected unless your doctor expresses an opinion that you are disabled, at least in part. Therefore, it is important to inform your physician of any problems you have working that result from your injuries.

6. **Failure to tell your doctor the truth.** Nothing will kill a personal injury claim quicker than lying about your injuries, disabilities, and other damages. It is extremely important to tell your doctor the truth during every appointment. On one hand, your doctor needs truthful facts to provide the proper treatment necessary to heal you. On the other hand, your doctor must believe you to report that your injuries are legitimate and caused by the accident. Finally, if a lie or exaggeration to your doctor is exposed by an insurance adjuster, investigator, or defense lawyer, your entire case will be dead on arrival with any judge or jury. Just tell the truth.

7. **Failure to use medication, equipment, or therapy as prescribed.** When it comes to prescription medications, orthotic devices, physical therapy, and other treatment recommendations, you should follow your doctor's advice to the letter. If medications cause side effects, simply tell your doctor, and your physician can suggest an alternative remedy. If you refuse to follow your doctor's advice, you will be playing into the insurance companies' hands and harming your case.

8. **Failure to discuss accident-related depression and anxiety.** Often, accident trauma can trigger problems such as depression, anxiety, or posttraumatic stress disorder (PTSD). These severe psychological conditions are every bit as real as the physical injuries caused by motor vehicle accidents. Moreover, when properly diagnosed and treated, psychological problems can add value to your case. Therefore, if you began feeling depressed, anxious, or otherwise psychologically distressed as a result of your accident and injuries, be sure to tell your doctors.

9. **Failure to take notes and keep a diary of your symptoms and treatment.** In every auto accident injury case, it is important to keep track of any and all injury symptoms as well as the resulting medical treatment. This information should be shared with your doctors and lawyer. However, due to the complexity of the auto accident claims process, many clients fail to keep track of these details. The best solution is to devise a system of taking notes, recording a diary, or otherwise documenting your medical problems and health care appointments. Get organized!

10. **Ending medical treatment too soon.** If you stop treating with your doctors before your injuries have completely healed or reached maximum medical improvement, you are making

a big mistake that will result in leaving much money on the table. The same should be said if you allow large gaps of time to accrue between medical treatment appointments. In short, insurance companies take the position that, if a person stops seeking medical treatment for an accident-related injury, then that person must be healed from injuries and pain free. Unfortunately, many judges and juries agree with that analysis. Therefore, as long as you continue to suffer any pain or other symptoms that affect your ability to function as a result of your accident injuries, you should continue to treat with your doctors until they discharge you.

11. **Discussing your lawsuit with your doctor.** In short, your doctor's job is to handle your medical treatment, and your lawyer's job is to handle your insurance claim or lawsuit. You should not allow your lawyer to interfere with your medical treatment or permit your doctor to frustrate your legal claims. In most situations, it is not a good idea to discuss your lawsuit or your lawyer with your doctor.

In summary, to help your doctors produce the quality reports you will need to win your case, you should do the following.

- Appear for all scheduled medical appointments.
- Tell your health care providers the truth about all symptoms, pain, discomfort, injuries, etc., resulting from the accident.
- Report any injury-related missed work or disability to your health care provider.
- Follow your doctor's advice.
- Keep your lawyer informed about your ongoing medical treatment.

CHAPTER 29
Independent Medical Examination

After you experience an automobile accident, you frequently seek medical attention when you are physically injured or psychological counseling when you experience mental distress. Though you may be unaware of it at the time of the examination, the records and opinions of these health care providers are frequently brought into court as evidence of your injuries and the extent of your suffering. You should be both open and honest with your health care provider. Often, this evidence is key to your case, especially when determining what kind of monetary award you will receive. However, your opposition in a trial will frequently want to counter the opinions and diagnoses of the health care providers from whom you sought treatment. To do this, they will ask you to submit to evaluation by a doctor hired by the defendant insurance company. They call it an Independent Medical Examination (IME). A better name for it would be DME: Defendant Medical Examination.

What is an IME?

An IME is a tool that your opponent can use to challenge the diagnoses or opinions of your treating doctor. The IME is actually not entirely "independent" because the IME doctor is usually chosen by the insurance company. This examination will generally involve the injuries that you sustained in the automobile accident. The doctor then provides diagnoses and opinions about your condition. As expected, these will often counter those of your doctor.

The general aim of your opponent when using an IME is to discredit the evidence submitted by your doctor. This provides your opponent with reasons to ask the judge or jury to lessen the amount of damages that you will receive for your physical or psychological injuries caused by the automobile accident. These kinds of examinations can be used to challenge the severity of your physical or mental injuries, the diagnosis you receive about your time of recovery, and many other aspects of your health care professional's opinions. Despite being titled "independent," these examinations usually have a defense-biased motive. Indeed, the IME doctor is actually a "hired gun" for the defendant insurance company.

> **FAST FACT**
> An IME is a tool the insurance company may use to challenge the findings of your treating doctor.

Who usually asks for an IME?

Generally, anyone you sue for monetary damages relating to a physical or mental injury would be interested compelling you to participate in an IME. In the context of a car accident, two types of people are the most likely to ask you to submit to additional examinations. The first is the person whom you are suing. This person will obviously have an interest in challenging your diagnoses or medical opinions because he or she will potentially have to pay the damages. The second are the insurance companies from which you seek monetary damages. As a practical matter, the lawyer hired by the defendant insurance company will typically schedule the IME.

Will my opponent ask for an IME?

This depends on many factors surrounding the case, but it is likely that your opponent will ask for an IME. The severity of your injury, the diagnosed causes of your injury, and the amount of monetary damages you seek in the case will all impact whether your opponent will ask for any additional examinations. Sometimes your opponent will not ask for any additional examinations. However, it is generally reasonable to assume that your opponent will ask for one in a personal injury case. While preparing for your lawsuit, you should be prepared to have to submit to an IME.

Will I be required to allow my opponent's medical professional examine me?

Usually, the answer is yes. You should be prepared to have to participate in an IME if you file a personal injury lawsuit.

How could an IME impact my case?

If your opponent at trial requests that you submit to an IME, the extent to which it will impact your case will vary. For example, it may be detrimental to your case if the judge or jury finds the IME particularly trustworthy or if they believe the new examiner is better qualified than your treating doctor. If this happens, this can impact your case in multiple negative ways.

First, it could potentially impact your success at trial. The extent of this impact can result in many different outcomes. For example, it can sometimes cause you to lose your entire case or part of it. Moreover, it could also call into question your health care professional's credibility, opinions, or diagnoses. Second, it could impact the amount of monetary compensation you will receive from your opponent in court. If the judge or jury questions the cause or extent of your injuries, the amount of monetary compensation you will recover will likely be lessened.

PART IV:
COMMERCIAL CONCERNS

CHAPTER 30
Commercial Truck Accidents

Accidents involving 18-wheelers and other big rigs can differ from run-of-the-mill motor vehicle accidents. If you are involved in an accident with an 18-wheeler or other commercial truck, it is important to understand some of the differences between these accidents and an accident with a personal-use vehicle—such as more severe impact resulting from collision with heavy trucks, greater insurance coverage available, and special rules that apply to trucking companies (like the federal motor carrier safety regulations). Some of the special rules that apply to 18-wheelers involve driver background checks, drug testing, driver logs, and hours of service, all of which can impact the outcome of a case.

> **FAST FACT**
> Special safety rules apply to 18-wheelers that involve driver background checks, drug testing, driver logs, hours of service, etc.

An accident involving a commercial truck can be much more disastrous than an accident between personal-use vehicles. A typical fully-loaded commercial truck, like an 18-wheeler or dump truck, can weigh 25 times as much as a typical car. Due to this weight disparity, most accidents involving 18-wheelers and other vehicles can result in more serious (or even fatal) injuries. For these reasons, semi-truck operators must follow a number of federal and state regulations, and are required to carry insurance with higher limits than standard personal-use vehicle drivers.

Commercial truck drivers are regulated by the U.S. Department of Transportation. They have a higher standard of duty and care than non-commercial drivers, because of the excessive danger involved with their accidents. Some of the regulations include: how much weight a big rig can haul; how long a driver can go without rest; and quality standards, which regulate the manufacturing and repair of commercial trucks. These are just a small fraction of the kinds of conduct regulated in the trucking business. With so many regulations, there is a chance that either the driver or trucking company violated one or more of the relevant laws or regulations when a commercial truck is involved in an accident. This is important because proof of violation of a statute or other regulation greatly increases the chance of showing that the commercial truck driver or company was at fault in the accident. The more someone is able to show the other party was at fault, the more likely that person is to prevail in a personal injury case, and the bigger the amount of damages he or she is likely to receive.

> **FAST FACT**
> A fully-loaded 18-wheeler can weigh 25 times as much as a typical car.

Although 18-wheeler trucks, semi-trailer vehicles, and other commercial trucks account for only 3–4% of all traffic on the roads in Louisiana, they are involved in about 9% of the total fatalities resulting from auto accidents. For these reasons, it is important to understand what constitutes a commercial truck accident and how the different rules and regulations can affect the outcome of an accident case involving a commercial truck or vehicle.

WHAT IS A COMMERCIAL TRUCK?

Accidents involving commercial trucks account for some of the most dangerous and deadly accidents in the country. As mentioned above, the outcome of a case can vary greatly if it involved a commercial truck as compared to a personal vehicle. The first thing to establish when figuring out if you have been in an accident with a commercial truck is to define what a "commercial truck" is. Although it may be obvious in many cases when one has been involved in an accident with a commercial truck, this is not always the case. Either way, it is important to understand what constitutes a commercial truck.

Generally, a commercial vehicle is any kind of vehicle that is used for a business or commercial purpose. A commercial vehicle could be a big truck (semis, tractor-trailers), a commercial bus, a van, or any other type of automobile used for commercial purposes. For the purpose of this chapter and the extra regulations which commercial vehicles are subject to, the main type of vehicles to consider are big commercial trucks, such as 18-wheelers or other tractor-trailers. It is important to know, however, that all types of commercial vehicles could be subject to additional regulations and insurance requirements. Technically, any vehicle that is used to carry freight or other commercial goods or is used for a business activity is a commercial vehicle, which may be subject to such regulations.

> **FAST FACT**
> Accidents involving commercial trucks account for some of the most dangerous and deadly accidents in the country.

Some common types of commercial vehicles to are:

- Semi trucks
- Tractor-trailers
- Delivery vehicles
- Commercial buses
- Hazmat carriers
- Tanker trailers
- Commercial vans

> **FAST FACT**
>
> A commercial vehicle is any kind of vehicle that is used for a business or commercial purpose.

Although there are many types of commercial vehicles and trucks (each with their own types of regulations and standards) the vehicles listed above are some of the main types of larger commercial transport vehicles to remember, because they are the ones most highly regulated by the Federal Department of Transportation. As defined by those regulations, the vehicle must be one that is used as part of a business and is involved in interstate commerce. It must also fit the following description to be considered a commercial vehicle:

- Weighs over 10,000 pounds
- Has a gross vehicle weight rating weight rating of over 10,000 pounds
- Is designed or used to transport 16 or more passengers not for compensation
- Is designed or used to transport 9 or more passengers for compensation
- Is transporting hazardous materials in a quantity requiring placards

Big trucks typically weigh anywhere from 10,000 to 100,000 pounds and can be as long as 60–70 feet. If the auto accident in question involved a vehicle that fit one of these descriptions, it is likely subject to more stringent federal commercial trucking laws and regulations.

COMMERCIAL TRUCKING DAMAGES

If someone is injured in an auto accident, that person is entitled to receive money from the person at fault in the form of damages. There are many different types of damages for which one can recover money. Because accidents involving commercial trucks can often be more severe, the law also allows for a greater potential for recovery. A commercial 18-wheeler may weigh up to 80,000 pounds with a full load, as opposed to personal car or truck, which may weigh closer to 3,000–4,000 pounds. When a large commercial truck has an accident with a regular car or truck, it may result in more severe injury or death. Because of the sheer mass of a commercial truck, as opposed to a personal vehicle, accidents involving them often result in much greater damages, for which an injured party may be able to recover.

COMMERICAL TRUCKING INSURANCE REQUIRMENTS

Just like all other drivers on the road, commercial truck drivers are required to carry a certain amount of minimum insurance coverage. The difference, however, is that state and federal regulations mandate higher insurance requirements on owners and drivers of large commercial trucks—as compared to regular personal-use vehicles—due to the severity of accidents in which large commercial trucks are involved. This is good for the injured party because it increases that person's chances of being able to recover the full amount of damages sought.

Individuals can be, and often are, uninsured or underinsured. In fact, 52% of drivers in Louisiana have coverage at or below the state-required minimum coverage for auto insurance. The amount of auto insurance the state legally requires a driver to carry is often not enough to cover all of the costs associated with an auto accident. When an individual has insufficient auto insurance to cover the costs related to an auto accident, that person is required to cover the additional cost out of his or her own pocket. This means that if you are in an auto accident with someone who is uninsured or underinsured, and that individual has no money of his or her own, it can be difficult to ever receive the money you are owed. Even if you obtain a legally binding judgment against another person for the cost of your auto accident, you may never actually receive that money if that person has no means to pay. It is for this reason that, for all practical purposes, cases will only be able to settle for an amount that is the maximum amount allowed by the defendant's insurance.

> **FAST FACT**
> State and federal regulations mandate higher insurance requirements on owners and drivers of large commercial trucks, as compared to regular personal-use vehicles.

Since commercial truck drivers, on the other hand, are required to carry higher levels of insurance than the average driver, it can be easier for people who are injured in those types of accidents to recover. The higher minimum policy requirements for commercial truckers mean that even if the driver or employer only carries the minimum amount, the plaintiff is less likely to be stuck with a small settlement, or one that does not truly encompass the full cost of his or her damages. Even though, on average, more damages are caused by commercial trucking accidents, there is also proportionally much more insurance coverage held by those commercial truckers. These insurance requirements are in place to protect those injured in truck accidents from truckers who cannot afford to pay damages to truck accident victims from their own pockets.

COMMERCIAL TRUCKING REGULATIONS

Determining who is at fault in an accident is the key element of any auto accident case. The party at fault is the party who will be responsible for payment of damages to the opposing party. Commercial truck drivers and commercial trucking companies are subject to a wide variety of laws, rules, and regulations that do not apply to non-commercial drivers, and determining who was at fault for the accident may hinge on a violation of one of those regulations. If the commercial driver or the driver's company did not follow the appropriate regulations, the driver and his or her company could be responsible for the damages resulting from the accident.

> **FAST FACT**
> Driver fatigue is the number one cause for truck accidents due to the error of the truck driver.

In order to increase the safety of trucks, to reduce the number of truck accidents, and to protect people from being involved in truck accidents, many trucking regulation laws exist. All trucks and truck drivers must carry commercial driver's licenses and adhere to the rules for the amount of rest a driver must have. They are also required to comply with maximum weight limits, standards for manufacturing and repair of trucks, and guidelines for the transportation of hazardous materials, as well as many other guidelines.

Driver fatigue is the number-one cause for truck accidents due to the error of the truck driver. Therefore, laws regarding the maximum number of hours that a truck driver can drive his or her truck have been established by the federal government to reduce truck driver fatigue, and in turn lower the number of truck accidents. Many truck drivers ignore these regulations, which can ultimately result in truck accidents. If it is found that a driver was in excess of his or her allowed maximum hours of operation by law, then this could help prove that the driver was at fault for the accident. Although this is just one example of a violation of trucking regulations, there are many others that you need to consider when reviewing a trucking accident.

Not all acts of truck driver negligence are related to specific trucking regulations, but when an accident has been caused by a truck driver's negligence, it is important to consider if any trucking regulations have also been violated. As stated before, if it can be proved that regulations were violated, the truck driver's negligence is easier to prove.

Some of the most common types of truck driver negligence are:

- Driver fatigue
- Texting/talking on a cell phone
- Eating and drinking
- Speeding
- Not obeying signs
- Driving while under the influence of alcohol or drugs
- Failure to yield the right of way
- Overweight/improper loading
- Falsified log books
- Improper truck maintenance
- Improper safety equipment
- Aggressive driving
- Failing to properly inspect trucks before, during, and after a route
- Continuing to drive despite adverse road conditions
- Violating the federal law on required sleep and rest time
- Inadequate truck driver training

Not only are most of these acts illegal, they can cause danger to the other drivers on the road. Although not all these types of driver negligence directly relate to a specific commercial trucking regulation, there are several types of evidence that can be collected to prove the truck driver involved in a truck accident was being negligent in his or her vehicle's operation at the time of the accident. Some of the key regulations to keep in mind, and ways to possibly prove the regulation was violated, are discussed in further detail below.

Federal Hours of Service Regulation

As stated before, truck driver fatigue is the number-one cause for truck accidents. This accounts for potentially 35–40% of all truck accidents. This is because truck drivers work long hours, have strict deadlines, and have to abide by rigorous schedules. Because of these factors, truck drivers can often push themselves when on the road to the point of fatigue to meet strict deadlines. Fatigue can mean lack of sleep, extreme tiredness, or exhaustion. When a truck driver is fatigued, it is possible for him or her to fall asleep at the wheel, which can lead to severe accidents.

> **FAST FACT**
> Hours of service regulations govern how many hours a commercial truck driver can drive over certain periods of time.

For these reasons, the federal government has passed "Hours of Service" regulations, which govern how many hours a commercial truck driver can drive over certain periods of time. The aim of these regulations is to ensure that commercial truck drivers get plenty of rest, and that the number of accidents involving commercial trucks will be therefore reduced.

Some of these regulations include the following:

- **An 11-hour driving limit.** No truck driver is allowed to drive more than 11 hours without taking 10 consecutive hours of rest between driving shifts.
- **A 14-hour on-duty limit.** Drivers are not allowed to be on-duty more than 14 hours, only 11 of which can be spent on the road.
- **60/70-hour week limit.** A driver may not drive more than 60 hours in 7 consecutive days, or 70 hours in 8 consecutive days. A new 7/8 consecutive day period can start only after 34 or more hours off.

Despite these regulations, not all truck drivers and trucking companies follow them, due to the high schedule demands and financial incentives of the job. There is much pressure to bend or break these rules in order to complete deliveries on time or ahead of schedule. Truck drivers are required to maintain a log book of their driving hours, so one of the first areas to investigate in a commercial truck accident is the driving log. It is important to know where the drivers have been in the days and hours preceding the accident and how many hours they had been driving to determine if they were in violation of any "Hours of Service" regulations. If it can be demonstrated that the driver was in violation of a regulation, then it will help establish that he or she was at fault in the accident.

> **FAST FACT**
> Driver fatigue accounts as much 35–40% of all truck accidents.

Truck Equipment Regulations

Another area of regulation involves the equipment used on a commercial truck. The parts and equipment on a large commercial vehicle are more highly regulated then those of a standard passenger vehicle. The Federal Motor Carrier Safety Administration (FMCSA) has made certain requirements for the maintenance and periodic inspections of large commercial trucks. Before drivers are allowed to hit the road, they are supposed to inspect their vehicles carefully. As per the FMCSA guidelines, a driver of a tractor-trailer is required to perform an inspection of his or her vehicle before, during, and after a trip, so as to know about and locate any defects in the truck and repair them prior to putting the truck back on the road.

Some of the inspection requirements a truck driver is required to comply with include:

- Examine the truck to note its condition and look for spills or leaks.
- Idle the engine to warm it up and listen for unusual noises.
- Check water levels in the engine and crankcase.
- Check that all lights and light signals are working properly.
- Check gauges to ensure they are showing proper readings.
- Check to ensure that windshield wipers, horn, and other emergency devices are operating.
- Check all wheels and tires to ensure they are properly secured and inflated.
- Check to ensure trailer is properly hooked up.
- Stop and inspect any problems a driver may notice while on the road.

A pre-trip and post-trip inspection for every tractor-trailer is required to be carried out daily by the truck driver or trucking company. This report should be kept on record, and any necessary repairs need to be made in a timely manner, prior to the vehicle returning to the road. In addition to periodic self-inspections, federal regulations require that commercial motor vehicles pass an annual inspection of their equipment and systems. This inspection must be done by an inspector certified by the Department of Transportation (DOT).

For this reason, it is important to examine inspection reports, maintenance logs, and the safety compliance materials that may have been issued by the trucking company, and to determine if the driver and company were in compliance with equipment and inspection regulations. Additionally, it would be beneficial for an accident investigator to examine the truck itself, if possible. That way the inspector can independently determine if there was any faulty or improper equipment on the vehicle.

Some of the equipment features to investigate are:

- Lamps, reflective devices, and electrical wiring
- Brakes and related monitoring systems
- Window construction and glazing
- Fuel systems
- Coupling devices and towing methods
- Tires
- Windshield wipers
- Seats and restraints
- Emergency equipment
- Cargo security devices
- Cab/body component

If any of these components are found to be damaged, defective, or missing, or the inspections of these components were not complied with, it may be possible to show they were a factor in the truck accident. Additionally, if the inspection and maintenance logs do not match what is on the truck, it can also show that the truck driver or trucking company were in violation of regulations. All of these things could help in proving their fault in the accident.

Licensing and Training Regulations

Driving a commercial truck requires a higher level of skill, knowledge, and experience than operating a regular personal vehicle. Therefore, a commercial truck driver is required to have a special truck-driving license in order to legally drive a large truck. This license is called a Commercial Motor Vehicle license, or CMV. If a driver does not have a CMV, or if it has been revoked for some reason, he or she is not legally allowed to drive a commercial truck. In order to obtain a CMV license, drivers must pass both a skills and knowledge test. Since commercial truck drivers are held to a higher standard than regular drivers, serious traffic violations—including, but not limited to, DWIs or DUIs—can affect a driver's ability to keep his or her CMV license. Drivers can also have their CMV license revoked for other major traffic infractions. Also, commercial truck drivers may be required to have special endorsements to drive certain kinds of commercial trucks.

> **FAST FACT**
> Driving a commercial truck requires a higher level of skill than a regular personal vehicle.

Some of the vehicles that require special endorsements are:

- Trucks with double or triple trailers
- Trucks with a tank
- Trucks carrying hazardous materials
- Passenger vehicles

A commercial truck driver is also required to undergo special training in order to drive tractor-trailers and semi-trucks. This type of training is called Longer Combination Vehicle (LCV) training. The purpose of this training is to establish minimum requirements for operators of longer combination vehicles. If a trucking company hires a driver who does not have a CMV license and LCV training, then the company could be liable in an accident for negligently hiring an unqualified driver. This is also true if a driver is driving a vehicle which requires a special endorsement to operate, but he or she does not have the required endorsement.

Truck drivers also need to pass a physical exam every two years, and failing this test would restrict their driving ability. Although the normal limit for what is considered driving under the influence of alcohol is a blood alcohol level (BAC) of .08%, truck drivers are not allowed to report for duty with a BAC of more than .02%. They cannot carry alcohol with them unless is a part of the cargo on their vehicle. Also, they are not allowed to consume any alcohol or any other type of drug that may impair their driving ability within 8 hours of their driving shift. Failure to comply with any of these trucking regulations can help establish liability on the part of the truck driver and/or trucking company for trucking accidents in which the driver was involved.

LIABLITY FOR COMMERCIAL TRUCKING ACCIDENTS

The most obvious parties to consider when determining who is at fault in a commercial trucking accident are the drivers of the vehicles, but these may not be the only parties who could be liable for damages in the accident. Since commercial trucks have a long list of factors that are involved in their safe operation and maintenance, there are many other parties to consider. Often the trucking company, as the employer of the driver, can be held liable for the accident—but they may not be the only ones either.

There are two main ways that an employer can be held responsible for an auto accident caused by one of its employees. The law doesn't necessarily require that the employer itself be at fault in any direct way; it states that employers are responsible for damage created by the actions of their employees if the action was part of the job they were employed to do. To know if the employer was responsible for the actions of its employee at the time an auto accident occurred, one has to consider two important factors that determine if this law applies.

The first is simply whether an employment relationship existed between the employer and employee. The second is whether the related act—in this case driving a motor vehicle at the time of the accident—was within the scope of that person's employment. Although both of these factors would likely be the case for most commercial trucking accidents, a more in-depth look at when and how employers can be held responsible for the actions of their employees can be found in this book's chapter entitled "Employer Liability."

The second factor is any action by the employer itself that may have contributed to the cause of the accident. Some of the ways an employer can be found liable by its own actions are through the negligent hiring of employees, negligent supervision of employees, and through their responsibility as owner of the vehicle. This type of liability is important, however, because it can be applied to non-employers as well. In commercial trucking accidents, there are many parties that have an impact whether the vehicle was suitably loaded, maintained, and operated on the road.

Some of the at-fault parties for a truck accident could include:

- The trucking company or motor carrier
- The truck repair company
- The truck manufacturer
- The owner of the truck's freight

- The loader of the truck's freight
- The last vehicle inspector
- The truck owner
- The truck owner's parent company
- The truck driver
- The driver's employer

Each of these parties could have a part in the operation of the truck, whether by being directly involved in its operation or by giving an endorsement that the driver and vehicle are fit for operation on the road. It is important to consider what role each of these parties had in the operation and deployment of the vehicle. If any of these parties were responsible for, or were the cause of, a violation of trucking regulations, they could be partially liable for an accident that was the result of that violation.

> **FAST FACT**
> A commercial trucking accident can be much more complicated than a regular personal vehicle accident.

PROVING A TRUCK ACCIDENT CASE

With higher damages at stake, so many potential defendants, and trucking regulations at play, a commercial trucking accident can be much more complicated than a regular personal vehicle accident. For this reason, it may also be harder to prove who exactly is at fault, and for what portion of the accident. The key to building a successful case starts with the accident investigation. This how the majority of the evidence is gathered. The three aspects of the case that must be most thoroughly investigated are the accident scene, the truck itself, and the related records.

An inspection of the truck is important for some of the reasons listed earlier in this chapter. The Federal Motor Carrier Safety Administration (FMCSA) has enacted certain requirements for the maintenance of commercial trucks, and it is important to find out if the vehicle was in compliance with these requirements. A list of items that you should check on the vehicle is listed above in the section on trucking equipment regulations. It is also important, as in any auto accident, to examine the accident scene.

Some things that should be documented to the greatest extent possible are:

- Date and time of the accident
- Where exactly the accident took place
- The position of the vehicles before and after the accident
- Photographs of the damage to the vehicles
- Photographs of traffic signs, obstructions, point of collision, and general scene
- Immediate recollection of the details of the accident
- Name and address and statements from anyone who witnessed the accident

The more information you can gather from the truck and the accident scene, the easier it will be to later prove the case against the defendants.

One of the biggest differences in proving a trucking accident case as compared to a personal vehicle case is in the other records and documentation that need to be collected. This can often be the key element in proving that a driver or trucking company was in violation of regulations. Therefore, obtaining and properly examining this information is crucial to the case.

Some of the records and other evidence that you should seek to

obtain include:
- Repair records
- Log books
- Cargo reports
- On-board recording data
- Inspection records
- Accident witnesses
- Electronic log systems
- Cell phone records
- Accident reports
- Crash Data Retrieval information
- Driver's license and certification information

Items such as log books can show if the driver was in excess of his or her mandatory operating requirements, and inspection records are helpful in showing if the vehicle was inspected at the proper intervals and if the necessary repairs were made. Cargo reports can indicate if the freight was in compliance with the load restrictions and other cargo regulations. These items are vital not just in proving the fault of the other party or parties, but in determining if there have been any violations of trucking regulations, and who was liable for them. This, in turn, goes a long way in proving the case against the driver or trucking company.

CHAPTER 31
Employer Liability

Did you know that if you are in an auto accident with an individual while he or she is on the job, that person's employer could be responsible for costs related to your accident? For example, if a person is in a car accident caused by a FedEx driver delivering packages, not only can the driver be held responsible, but the company he works for (in this case FedEx) could be responsible as well. This fact can actually go a long way in determining the outcome of your case.

Individuals can be, and often are, uninsured or underinsured. In fact, 52% of drivers in Louisiana carry coverage at or below the state-required minimum for auto insurance. The amount of auto insurance the state legally requires a driver to carry is often not enough to cover all of the costs associated with an auto accident. When an individual has insufficient auto insurance to cover the costs related to an auto accident, that person is required to cover the additional cost out of his or her own pocket.

> **FAST FACT**
> If the person who caused your accident was on the job, his or her employer could be held responsible for your damages.

The costs related to an auto accident can be significant, especially if there are injuries involved. This means if you are in an auto accident with someone who is uninsured or underinsured, and that person has no money of his or her own, it can be difficult to ever receive the compensation you are owed. Even if you obtain a legally binding judgment against another person for the cost of your auto accident, you may never actually receive that money if that person has no means to pay. There are thousands of auto accident victims who go unpaid in this manner every year.

Businesses, however, usually have the means to pay when an auto accident involving an employee occurs. A company such as FedEx, which employs thousands of drivers all over the world, understands that it is inevitable that many of them will be involved in auto accidents. Therefore, it is highly likely FedEx itself could be responsible for the costs associated with those accidents. For this reason, businesses usually make sure they have more than sufficient insurance to cover the accidents caused by their employees.

Although recovering funds owed to you by an insurance company can be a long, complicated, and frustrating process, it is much easier than recovering money from an individual who simply does not have any. Additionally, should the costs of your accident exceed the driver's auto insurance coverage, the average business (even a small business) has more assets available than the average individual to cover those costs.

With all of that in mind, it is critical to determine if there could be an employer responsible for costs related to your accident. In some instances, as with the FedEx driver, it may seem obvious there is an employer that should be considered as a possible defendant, but this is not always the case. What if the FedEx driver was on his lunch break at the time the accident occurred? What about a construction worker sent on an errand by his boss to purchase extra supplies from the store who is driving his personal pickup truck? What about a receptionist who is picking up copies for the office, but stops to get

> **FAST FACT**
> Businesses usually carry much more liability insurance coverage than individuals.

herself a cup of coffee on the way back? These are all situations in which it is not obvious whether the employer is responsible or not. However, the extent of the employer's responsibility can be determined by keeping a few simple factors in mind.

There are two main criteria by which an employer can be held responsible for an auto accident caused by one of its employees. The first is an action by the employer itself that may have contributed to the cause of the accident. For example, if FedEx hired someone who did not have a valid driver's license, and that driver caused an auto accident, then FedEx's decision to hire someone who did not know how to operate a motor vehicle would have contributed to the cause of the accident. In that situation, FedEx acted in a direct manner that was partially responsible for the accident.

The second doesn't necessarily require the employer itself to be at fault in any direct way. The law states that employers are responsible for damage created by the actions of their employees if the action was part of the job they were employed to do. In the case of the FedEx driver, driving the FedEx truck is obviously part of the job he or she was employed to do. If the driver runs into someone's parked car while delivering packages, then the accident resulted as part of the job he or she was hired to do, and the employer, FedEx, is likely be responsible for costs associated with that accident.

> **FAST FACT**
> An employer can be held responsible even if employee was driving a personal vehicle, as long as the employee was doing his or her job.

Employer liability only applies if the employee is actually in the process of doing something for the employer at the time when the accident occurred. For example, if a receptionist is sent to the store to pick up copies for the office and got into an accident on the way, her employer could be responsible because she was acting on its behalf. If, instead, the receptionist decided to stop and buy herself a cup of coffee on the way back and she gets into an accident in the process, she is no longer acting on behalf of the employer. Therefore, her employer may not be responsible.

To know if the employer was responsible for the actions of its employee at the time an auto accident occurred, one has to consider two important factors that determine if this law applies. The first is simply whether an employment relationship existed between the employer and employee. The second is whether the related act—in this case, driving a motor vehicle at the time of the accident—was within the scope of that person's employment.

THE EMPLOYMENT RELATIONSHIP

Since employers can be responsible for the actions of their employees, the first thing to consider is simply if an individual was employed at the time of the accident. This on its own does not mean the person's employer is at all responsible, but it is the first and most basic fact that must be determined. Obviously, if the person was unemployed at the time of the accident, there can be no employer who is also responsible for it. If the individual was driving a company vehicle, such as a FedEx truck, it may be easy to determine. It should, however, be established in EVERY auto accident whether or not the other party was employed at the time the accident happened. Even if the person was driving his or her personal vehicle, his or her employer could still be responsible for costs related to the accident. If the individual was driving a personal vehicle for a purpose related to his or her employment, such as a construction worker going to the store to pick up more supplies, his employer could still be responsible for an auto accident the construction worker caused, since he was running the errand as part of his job.

Usually, determining if someone is employed is not difficult, but that is not always the case. Most of the time someone is employed by a company as a payroll employee, meaning that person is employed either part-time or full-time and paid on an hourly or salary basis. In those cases it is usually relatively easy to determine employment. While this type of employment certainly would establish the requisite employment relationship for employer responsibility, it is not the only kind. Employers can hire individuals on a more temporary or contract basis, and this may not be sufficient to create the proper type of employment relationship wherein the employer would be held responsible for an individual's actions.

It is important to be aware that employers are not normally responsible for the actions of an independent contractor hired by the company, except under unique circumstances. Independent contractors are deemed to be self-employed, since they generally do not operate under the direct supervision of the party hiring them. Therefore, employers are not responsible for their actions unless the employer exercises an exceptionally great deal of control over the independent contractor. If this is in fact the case, then it is possible an employment relationship is still created. An employer can also be responsible for the actions of an independent contractor if there is an unusually high amount of danger involved in the activity for which the contractor is hired.

> **FAST FACT**
> Employers are not normally responsible for the actions of an independent contractor hired by the company.

Some factors to consider in determining whether an employment relationship has been created between an employer and a contractor are:

- Does the employer have the right to exercise control?
- Is there a contract between the employer and contractor?
- Did the employer or did the contractor choose the means of accomplishing the work?
- Is the object of the contract a particular piece of work for a set price?
- Does the task involve an inherently dangerous activity?
- Did the employer authorize work to be performed in an unsafe way?
- Does the employer try to avoid responsibility for a dangerous activity?

Whether the individual is a regular payroll employee or an independent contractor in one of these special circumstances, it is important to first establish if the other party was employed at the time of the accident. Once this is established, then whether or not the activity—in this case, driving a motor vehicle at the time of the accident—was within the scope of the employment can be evaluated.

SCOPE OF THE EMPLOYMENT

The second (and, in some ways, more important) factor to consider when determining employer responsibility is whether the act—in this case, operating a motor vehicle at the time of the accident—was performed as part of the employee's job. Employers are responsible for the acts of their employees if the act was within the scope of their employment. If we go to the example of the FedEx driver, driving the FedEx truck is most certainly within the scope of the driver's employment. A construction worker sent to pick up paint, lumber, or other supplies, who gets in an accident on the way, would likely be considered to be within the scope of his employment while he was driving, since he was performing this task for the purpose of his job.

It is important, however, to understand employers are NOT responsible for actions of employees engaged in a "frolic or detour" from their employment responsibilities. To what extent employees can deviate from their responsibilities before they are considered no longer in the scope of their employment is very dependent on the facts. This does mean, however, that if a receptionist went ten minutes across town to get a cup of coffee from her favorite coffee shop on her way to pick up copies, when the copy shop was only two blocks from her office, that her employer may not be at all responsible for an accident that occurs when she is traveling to or from the coffee shop. The law says if an employee's deviation from her employment activities is substantial, then she is no longer in the scope of her employment, and therefore the employer is not responsible for her actions—namely the auto accident she may have caused.

Some factors to consider which help determine if the employee was in the scope of his or her employment include:

- Time and place of the employee's action
- Purpose of the employee's action
- Employer's control over how action of the employee was performed
- The employee's duty to the employer to perform the action
- The employer's expectation for the employee
- The benefits received by the employer due to the employee's action
- How the employee's actions relate to the employer's business

While there is no hard-and-fast rule to determine if an employee's action was in the scope of his or her employment, there are many situations where it is not difficult to establish that a driver was performing a duty related to his or her job at the time of an accident. This is why it is important to always keep in mind possible employers as defendants. When there is an employment relationship in existence between a party involved in an accident and an employer, and that party was in the scope of his or her employment at the time of the accident, it is likely there will be two proper defendants in the case: the party involved in the accident and his or her employer.

WHEN EMPLOYERS ARE RESPONSIBLE BY THEIR OWN ACTIONS

The discussion above relates to employers being responsible for auto accidents when they themselves have not directly contributed to the accident, except through the actions of their employees. As mentioned earlier, however, there are situations in which an employer can be held responsible for an accident based directly on its own fault. Although this is a less-common means by which to establish employer responsibility when dealing with auto accidents, it can still occur, especially when dealing with accidents involving companies that employ commercial drivers. One of the most common ways to find an employer responsible through its own actions is based on a company's negligent hiring practices or negligent supervision of its employees. Another way is if the business is the owner of a vehicle that was in an accident (*i.e.*, a company vehicle is involved in an auto accident).

Negligent Hiring of Employees

Employers have a lot of discretion in deciding which employees they should hire to work for them. When the job involves a dangerous activity, such as driving a motor vehicle, they have a duty to exercise a certain amount of care to hire employees who will not unnecessarily put third parties at high levels of risk. This means that when hiring someone, employers have the responsibility to make sure the person is reasonably qualified for the job, especially if that person will be performing a job that can be dangerous to others. For example, when a company hires someone they know will be driving a company vehicle, the employer has a duty to make sure the employee is a safe driver. There are several ways they can attempt to do this. First, if the employee is going to be driving a commercial vehicle, the employer should make sure the employee has a commercial driver's license. The employer should also make sure the license has not been suspended and is in good standing. Additionally, it would be good practice to look into driving records to check for a history of accidents and traffic violations, as well as perform drug tests.

In a situation where a company hired a person to be a driver for them and did not perform some of these basic procedures, such as ensuring someone driving a commercial vehicle had a commercial driver's license, the company can be found responsible for negligent hiring practices of their employees. Since it can be argued that the employer's actions of putting an unqualified individual on the road directly contributed to the occurrence of an accident, they could be considered at least partially responsible for that accident.

Negligent Supervision of Employees

Employers also have the duty to properly supervise their employees, especially when their jobs involve dangerous activities like operating a motor vehicle. Negligent supervision is another way in which an employer can be held responsible for accidents of its employees based on its own direct fault. Companies that employ drivers should have safety policies in place and make sure all of their drivers comply with safety laws. For example, if an employer operates a commercial trucking company, the employer should make sure that drivers abide by relevant state and federal laws, that cargo is properly weighed and loaded, and that other safety procedures are followed.

If an employer does not closely supervise its employees to make sure they are following proper safety guidelines, obtaining proper training when necessary, and generally exercising reasonable care in doing their job, then that employer could be responsible for accidents caused by its employees. For example, if a trucking accident occurs because cargo was not properly loaded and came loose in transit, and the company's employees were never trained on how to load the cargo properly or not supervised to ensure it was being done correctly, it could be found that the employer's actions (or in this case lack of actions) were a cause of the accident. Therefore, the employer can be found responsible for the accident based on its own negligent supervision of employees.

EMPLOYER RESPONSIBILITY AS OWNER OF THE VEHICLE

Owners of vehicles can also be responsible for accidents their vehicles were involved in even if they were not the driver at the time of the accident. This means employers can be responsible in situations where a company vehicle was involved in a car accident. Even if the employee is off duty or performing a task outside of the scope of his or her employment, they could still be partially responsible for the accident as owner of the vehicle. For example, pizza delivery drivers often times will use their personal vehicles for their delivery jobs. This means if they are not delivering at the time of an accident then their employer is likely not responsible. FedEx delivery drivers, on the other hand, drive FedEx trucks owned by the company. This means the employer could be responsible for accidents involving its trucks no matter when they occurred and who was driving them

It is important to know that for an employer to be considered responsible for an accident simply based on the fact it is the owner of the vehicle involved, there are additional circumstances that likely need to have occurred, but just the fact that a company owns the vehicle involved auto accident could be enough to make them a defendant in the case.

INTENTIONAL ACTS OF EMPLOYEES

It is important to note that when considering if an employer is responsible for the actions of one of its employees, this standard usually only applies to **accidents** caused by the employee. An employer will typically not be held responsible for intentionally harmful acts committed by its employees. This means that if an employee decides he wants to deliberately run someone over with his car, even while on the job, the employer won't likely be responsible for it. The only time an employer could be responsible for the intentionally harmful acts of one of its employees is when the act is so closely connected in time and place to the scope of the employment that it is caused by something attributable to the employer's business. For example, if an employee deliberately ran someone over with his car right after work because he had just been fired, there is a chance the employer could be partially responsible because the circumstances are closely related its business. However, this would still be highly unlikely and require more relevant factors for the employer to have any legal responsibility. Usually if an employee is deliberately trying to hurt another person, this is outside of the scope of his or her employment, since no job would under any circumstances require such an action. Therefore, employers are most likely not responsible for these actions of their employees, regardless of the other circumstances.

> **FAST FACT**
> An employer will usually not be responsible for intentionally harmful acts committed by its employees.

To summarize, there are many situations in which an employer can be responsible for the costs associated with an auto accident. It is therefore crucial to determine if the other party was employed at the time of the accident and was within the scope of his or her employment, or if the person's employer directly contributed to cause of the accident in any way.

CHAPTER 32
Workers' Compensation

When you are involved in an automobile accident while you are on the job, you should seek whatever medical care is necessary. You should also alert the proper authorities as you normally would. However, getting in an accident while working brings more factors into consideration—namely, workers' compensation. Injuries you receive resulting from an automobile accident while on the job will usually bring workers' compensation implications into the situation, and these can have big impacts. This chapter will outline the basics of how an automobile accident and workers' compensation can be intertwined.

> **FAST FACT**
> Workers' compensation does not allow for recovery of damages beyond medical expenses and lost wages.

Workers' compensation is a state-mandated program in which most employers must participate. In the case that an employee is injured on the job or has some kind of work-related illness, workers' compensation provides compensation to that employee for his or her injury. Workers' compensation does not allow for recovery of damages beyond your medical expenses and lost wages. Therefore, injuries in a work-related car accident do not allow for the same recovery you can get in most personal injury suits, such as damages for pain and suffering. In Louisiana, workers' compensation shields employers from lawsuits brought by their employees on grounds other than intentional acts which were meant to cause injury, such as battery or assault.

If you are driving a vehicle within the course and scope of your employment, an accident that occurs while you are driving the vehicle is likely covered by workers' compensation. Actions in the course and scope of your employment can include activities such as driving from one worksite to another for work purposes, running errands for your employer, or driving because it is an integral part of your job. Odds are, if you are driving for at least a somewhat work-related purpose, any injury you experience in an accident will be covered by workers' compensation. Though this can limit your ability to recover against your employer, you could potentially have other parties at fault through which you could recover. These are outlined below.

> **FAST FACT**
> If you were within the course and scope of your employment at the time of your accident, you are likely covered by workers' compensation.

FILING CLAIMS AGAINST THIRD PARTIES

While you can usually only recover workers' compensation payments from your employer in the case of an automobile accident on the job, you may be able to recover more damages through third parties who are at fault. There are an unlimited amount of factors that could have led to your accident. For example, if you are involved in a collision, you can sue the other driver if he or she is at fault in the accident. Additionally, if you were a passenger in the car and not the driver, you can likely sue the driver for your injury if he is not an employee or co-worker. These are only a few of the numerous cases wherein you could sue a third party for an accident that occurred on the job. The ability to take a third party to court could dramatically increase the amount of damages you receive for the injury.

The reason why many people seek to sue a third party is that these third-party suits are generally going to be governed by personal injury law, not workers' compensation law. Therefore, the victim in a car accident could recover what is known as general damages, such as pain and suffering, as opposed to merely recovering medical bills and lost wages through workers' compensation. In short, suits against third parties can get you more money to which you are entitled.

Taking this into consideration, it is important for you to be observant after an automobile accident while you are on the job. Sometimes it is obvious that a third party played a substantial role in the accident and should be sued. For example, if you are struck from behind by a driver who failed to properly brake, that driver would be presumed to be at fault under Louisiana law. However, sometimes the assignment of responsibility is not so clear. Whenever you are involved in a work-related automobile accident, make sure to discuss with your attorney all parties that may be at fault in the accident. Doing so could lead to fairer settlement or ruling for you.

There are many ways that a third-party claim can impact both the overall damages you receive from the accident and your workers' compensation benefits. This section outlines some of these impacts, as well as the technicalities involved in suing a third party. These are important caveats to the law, and you should consider them before potentially suing a third party in a work-related accident.

How Your Third-Party Case Impacts Your Employer

The potential downside of a third-party suit in a work-related automobile accident is that your employer will usually receive some (potentially all) of your damages awarded in court. When you are awarded damages in court or in a settlement, your employer will be reimbursed for the workers' compensation payments they previously made to you before you receive any of your compensation from the settlement or the court's ruling. Additionally, if the amount of the award is higher than the amount of workers' compensation benefits you have already received, your employer will receive a credit for this. The effect of this credit is that your employer does not have to pay any more workers' compensation benefits until you surpass the amount of the court's award or settlement. In the case that the amount is less than the amount of workers' compensation benefits you have already received, your employer will get the entire amount. This rule applies to both trials and settlements.

This should not act as a deterrent to you filing a third party suit, especially if you believe you will receive a large sum from the court. It is simply a factor to consider when planning to file suit.

Moody Fees

Sometimes both you and your employer may sue a third party for the injuries that you have incurred. If this is the case, your employer will be potentially responsible for some of the attorney's fees that you incur as part of the suit. These are called Moody fees, and the practical effect of these fees is that up to one-third of your employer's recovery from a case can be taken from the employer's recovery in order to pay for your attorney. When the court makes its decision on what to award you, it will decide the amount of the employer's recovery that will be taken. Keep in mind that one-third is the maximum that the employer will have to contribute; however, they might pay considerably less.

Important Technicalities

First, when you decide to sue a third party in the case of a work-related automobile accident, you must notify your employer of the suit. This notification has to be in writing. The purpose of this notification is to allow the employer to decide whether or not to sue the third party as well. Usually such a suit would be filed because the third party caused expenses for the employer (*i.e.*, the employer has had to pay you workers' compensation benefits).

Second, when you decide to settle, you must notify your employer in writing. Once you offer this notification, you must also receive approval from your employer in writing in order to settle. If you settle without notifying your employer and receiving approval, you will be ineligible for future workers' compensation benefits from your employer.

CHAPTER 33
Products Liability

When you are involved in an automobile accident, frequently you ponder such issues as determining who is at fault, and what caused the accident. These are valid questions, but sometimes fault can be allocated to parties that were not seemingly directly involved in the accident. This is the case with products liability. You may have a right to sue the manufacturer of your automobile or its parts (or any other automobile or parts involved in the accident) if the automobile or part itself was one of the contributing factors that caused your accident. After an automobile accident, try to remember any abnormalities you experienced while handling your automobile. These may point you in the direction of a potential defect that led to the accident.

FAST FACT
You may have a right to sue a manufacturer if the automobile or its parts caused your accident.

This chapter outlines what exactly a products liability lawsuit is, whether you would likely have a strong case in your accident, and what are some common parts of automobiles that lead to products liability cases.

Generally, you can sue for products liability when you are using a product for its intended purpose, and some kind of manufacturing or production defect caused it to malfunction and injure or otherwise cause harm to you. In Louisiana, the Louisiana Products Liability Act provides various avenues through which you can sue for products liability. First, the law explains that you can only sue for products liability when a characteristic of the product was "unreasonably dangerous," and it caused your injury while you used the product for a "reasonably anticipated use." The law further explains that there are four kinds of "unreasonably dangerous" characteristics.

You must meet one of the following criteria to have a strong case.

- The product is unreasonably dangerous in construction or composition.
- The product is unreasonably dangerous in design.
- The product is unreasonably dangerous because an adequate warning about the product has not been provided.
- The product is unreasonably dangerous because it does not conform to an express warranty of the manufacturer.

Additionally, you must prove that this characteristic existed when the product left the manufacturer or that it resulted from a modification the manufacturer could have foreseen. In the case of an automobile accident, you should consider filing a products liability suit if you were driving a car responsibly and a product flaw of the automobile caused it to malfunction and injury you. There are numerous parts of your car that can lead to this kind of lawsuit. The following sections will explain common sources of products liability suits in automobile accidents.

> **FAST FACT**
> You can sue for products liability when you are using a product for its intended purpose, and some kind of manufacturing or production defect caused it to malfunction and injure or otherwise cause harm to you.

TIRE DEFECTS

Defective tires have been involved in several major products liability cases, and the likelihood that defective tires will cause automobile accidents again is high. An unfortunate reality is that victims of automobile accidents frequently do not realize that their tires were a contributing factor to or the direct cause of their accident. While there are many kinds of tire defects that can cause serious automobile accidents, the most common is tread separation.

Tread separation has been a part of numerous products liability lawsuits. It can be very dangerous, especially at high speeds. Tread separation occurs when the tread of the tire separates from the tire itself. This can result in a blowout, loss of control of the automobile, rollover, or other dangerous outcomes. When this kind of accident occurs, you should consider filing a products liability lawsuit. Make sure to check your tires to see if you have any visible signs of tread separation when you are involved in an accident.

In addition to tread separation, there are other tire defects that could lead to an automobile accident. For example, improper installment of a tire by the manufacturer could cause the tire to separate from the wheel, leading to an accident. An improperly designed tire could also lead to the same outcome. While the potential kinds of tire defects are limitless, it is important for you to inspect your tires after an accident and discuss any irregularities you see with your lawyer. This could lead to you recovering more damages for your injuries.

AIRBAG DEFECTS

Airbags are obviously an integral part of any safe automobile. However, an improperly designed airbag can be harmful. In the case of an automobile accident, a defective airbag can cause traumatic injuries or even death. The following section outlines a few common airbag defects that you may experience in an automobile accident. If you do experience these dangerous defects, you may be able to recover under a products liability lawsuit.

Untethered Airbags

In the case of an automobile accident, airbags should stop expanding at a certain point. Airbags should not slam into the face or body of the automobile occupants. One major way to prevent this kind of incident is tethering the airbag. A tether will stop the airbag before it expands too much, and it will also usually guide the airbag in the proper direction. To save money, many manufacturers in the past have not tethered airbags. This has led to numerous injuries, as well as lawsuits centered on these untethered airbags. When you are in an automobile accident and you believe you were injured by your airbag, make sure to check whether it was tethered. If it was not, you should inform your lawyer of this immediately.

Airbag Sensor Defects

The timing of when your airbag deploys in an automobile accident is usually determined by sensors in the car that determine when the best time is to deploy. While these sensors are usually reliable, there are cases where injuries are caused because an airbag either deployed too early or too late. This kind of defect can obviously cause serious injuries, so it is important to look into whether the sensors in your automobile were properly calibrated and functioning. If injuries in your car accident were caused by your airbag, you should definitely try to determine if a sensor defect caused the airbag to deploy too early or too late.

Airbag Folding and Venting Problems

Sometimes, a defect in the design or the folding of airbags can cause injury to the victim of an automobile accident. These design defects are usually caused by the manufacturer's folding the airbags in an improper way before their insertion into the automobile, or defectively designing the vents from which gas can escape the airbag. If you believe that your injuries could potentially have stemmed from your airbag, make sure to ask your lawyer to look into whether there was a folding or vent defect.

SEAT BELT DEFECTS

When you are involved in an automobile accident, a defective seat belt could lead to several potential injuries. Pinpointing whether the seat belt itself is the cause of the injury can be very difficult. Obviously, seat belts are an integral part of a safe vehicle, so having a well-functioning, safe seat belt in your vehicle is important. The following are a few of the most common seat belt defects in automobile accidents.

Webbing Rips and Tears

The webbing of the seat belt itself is usually very strong and should be able to withstand the force of an accident. However, webbing can tear, leaving the occupant of the automobile with little to no seat belt protection. In these cases, the result may be as though the individual was not wearing a seat belt at all. The injuries that result from these defects can be very tragic. Therefore, make sure to inspect whether your seat belt tore or was ripped during your automobile accident. This is one of the more visible and easy-to-detect seat belt defects.

Unlatching

As the name implies, unlatching is when the force of an automobile accident victim on the seatbelt causes the seat belt to unlatch. This, like webbing rips and tears, can essentially neutralize any benefits received by wearing a seat belt. This kind of malfunction will likely cause injury. When you are involved in an automobile accident and you believe that unlatching occurred, it can sometimes be hard to prove. However, if you know that you always wear a seat belt, but your injuries suggest that you were not wearing one at the time of the accident, this may be a strong indicator of unlatching. If you have any reason to believe that unlatching was the cause of your injuries, be sure to inform your lawyer of this and investigate it further with him or her.

False Latching

False latching is when you believe that your seat belt is secured, but it is actually unlatched. It can have the feeling of being securely in place even though you are completely unbuckled in reality. When this happens, it is not your fault that you believed that a seemingly-latched seat belt was, in fact, latched even though it was not. Like unlatching, this kind of defect can lead to neutralizing the safety benefits of your seat belt. If you believe that you have experienced this kind of seat belt defect, make sure to inform your lawyer.

Other Seat Belt Defects

There are many other kinds of seat belt defects that can cause injuries during an automobile accident; some will be briefly discussed here. First, retractor failure is a defect that can happen when your seat belt locks up too early or too late whenever you are involved in an automobile accident. This usually happens because of some kind of defect in the retractor of your seat belt, which is the mechanism that causes a seat belt to lock up whenever you exert force upon it. Whenever there is retractor failure, as mentioned above, the seat belt can lock up too early, lock up too late, or not lock up at all. This over-restraint or lack of restraint can lead to injury. Additionally, the placement and design of where the seat belt goes in the car can cause the seat belt to be ineffective in some situations. For example, a properly placed seat belt for a low-speed accident may not work well in the case of a high-speed accident or a rollover.

There are many kinds of seat belt defects that can cause you injury during your automobile accident. The above are some of the more common and serious defects, but there are many more. When you are involved in an automobile accident and you believe that your seat belt may be at least partially to blame for your injuries, make sure to inform your lawyer of this and document any reasons why you believe this is the case.

BRAKE DEFECTS

Brakes can also have defects that can be very dangerous. Whenever brakes are defective, they can cause accidents that may not actually be your fault. In fact, if you can prove that the brake system is what caused your automobile accident, you can sometimes avoid blame for an accident altogether. There are several kinds of brake defects that can cause an accident. Brake failure is a common source, and this can be caused by issues with the automobile such as a lack of power supply to the brakes or faulty parts. Moreover, brakes can lock up due to a number of factors that may not be your fault. Though it can be difficult to initially pinpoint exactly what caused your brake failure, the driver will frequently be able to tell that the brakes were faulty.

ACCELERATOR DEFECTS

If you are involved in an accident that was caused by your automobile accelerating when you were not pressing the accelerator, you may have a car with an accelerator defect. These kinds of defects have gotten a substantial amount of media coverage lately, and they can lead to accidents. While a high-speed incident involving an accelerator malfunction is dangerous, lower-speed malfunctions can be equally dangerous in some situations. If you believe that your accident was caused by an accelerator malfunction, make sure to research other cases that may have involved your make and model of car, and also to inform your lawyer of this as well.

OTHER MISCELLANEOUS DEFECTS

The above are some common defects that you find in automobiles, but there are still several other defects that can cause an automobile accident or injury. For example, a poorly designed SUV may lead to rollover if its center of gravity is too high. While not all automobile defects may be obvious, if you believe that a defect may have caused your accident, you should always look further into the matter. A little research can go a long way in this kind of litigation.

APPENDIX:
LEGAL LAGNIAPPE

Frequently Asked Questions

What's the minimum liability insurance coverage required by law in Louisiana?

Louisiana law requires at least the following minimal automobile liability insurance coverage:

- $15,000 coverage for bodily injury to any one person
- $30,000 coverage for total bodily injury for all people per accident
- $25,000 coverage for property damage (*e.g.*, vehicle repairs)

Can I recover for auto accident injuries and other damages if I didn't have car insurance?

Louisiana's "no pay, no play" law does not allow uninsured motorists to collect the first $15,000 in personal injuries and the first $25,000 in property damages, regardless of who was at fault in the accident. This law makes it more difficult for a person to recover damages related to their auto accident from another person's insurance company if they do not have an auto insurance policy themselves.

How can I protect myself before an accident?

Listen closely—this is the most important advice we give our clients. The single best way to protect your family from dangerous drivers before an accident occurs is to purchase as much uninsured/underinsured motorist bodily injury insurance coverage, also known as UM insurance, as you can afford. UM insurance is a contract between you and your car insurance company that protects your family against damages caused by uninsured motorists, underinsured motorists, and hit-and-run drivers.

How can I protect myself after an accident?

There are several simple steps you can take to protect your rights after a motor vehicle accident:

- Get medical treatment.
- Preserve accident and injury evidence.
- Refuse to talk to the other driver's insurance adjuster.
- Contact the right personal injury lawyer.

How can I get my car fixed without involving a lawyer?

Here are seven simple steps to recover for your property damage on your own:

1. Document the damage.
2. Obtain information and police report.
3. Notify insurance companies of claim.
4. Get a body shop estimate.
5. Submit your claim in writing.
6. Calendar the 30-Day bad faith deadline.
7. Read "7 Simple Steps to Fix Your Car Accident Property Damage."

How can I tell if I have a good case?

If you can answer "yes" to the following questions, you probably have a valuable car accident personal injury case:

1. Was the accident someone else's fault?
2. Was there visible damage to your vehicle?
3. Were your injuries promptly treated by a doctor?
4. Did your accident occur less than a year ago?
5. Is liability or UM insurance available to cover your claim?

If your accident was someone else's fault, your vehicle damage was noticeable, your injuries were promptly and properly treated, your accident happened less than a year ago, and adequate insurance coverage exists, you probably have a good case. However, because each case is different, you should contact a lawyer soon to discuss your case in more detail.

What are the most common mistakes that can ruin my auto accident personal injury case?

These are "The Top 5 Mistakes That Can Wreck Your Auto Accident Claim":

1. Not getting enough information at the accident scene.
2. Giving a recorded statement to other side's insurance company.
3. Waiting too long to see a doctor.
4. Waiting too long to hire a lawyer.
5. Lying about accidents, injuries, income, or activity levels.

Should I go to the doctor after my car accident?

Yes. If you have been injured, seek medical attention as soon as possible after your auto accident. Perhaps the worst mistake you can make to wreck your auto accident injury case is to avoid or delay medical treatment. You should, of course, see the health care provider of your own choosing: emergency room, urgent care clinic, after-hours clinic, family doctor, orthopedist, neurologist, chiropractor, etc. Just do not wait until it is too late.

What can an experienced personal injury lawyer do for me following my car accident?

In a nutshell, your attorney should maximize your financial recovery and minimize your stress. Your lawyer should handle the hassle of the insurance claims process. He or she should protect your rights every step of the way, even if the odds are stacked in favor of giant insurance companies like Allstate, State Farm, and GEICO. Your attorney should do this by using his or her personal injury law experience to level the playing field between you and the Goliath insurance company standing in your way. Finally, your lawyer should do the following:

- Answer all your questions and guide you through this difficult process.
- Collect and organize the information and documents needed to build your case.
- Force the insurance companies to play by the rules and treat you fairly.
- Help you get the money you need to recover and move forward.

How much does an experienced personal injury lawyer cost?

In personal injury and wrongful death cases, lawyers typically charge a contingent fee. Under this arrangement, attorneys' fees are only paid if a favorable result is achieved (*i.e.*, "no win, no fee"). This means that the lawyer requires no up-front money from the client, but instead the attorney gets a percentage of the eventual recovery, typically 33%–40% of any settlement or judgment collected. The contingent fee arrangement provides access to the courts for victims of others' fault who cannot otherwise afford to pay attorneys' fees. Contingent fees also provide a powerful motivation for attorneys to work diligently with a results-oriented emphasis.

How can I choose the right lawyer for my personal injury case?

Not all attorneys are created equal. The right lawyer could be the difference between winning and losing. You can make a smart, informed decision quickly if you use common sense and follow a few straightforward guidelines:

1. Do your homework.
2. Examine experience.
3. Question qualifications.
4. Research reputation.
5. Interview attorneys.

For a more details, check out "5 Easy Steps for Choosing the Right Lawyer."

What am I required to prove to win my personal injury case?

At the most basic level, all you need to prove is that you suffered injuries that were caused by someone else's fault. Of course, it rarely remains that simple once giant insurance companies and their high-powered lawyers get involved. Under Louisiana law, you must prove the following six things in order to prevail:

1. The party at fault had a duty to behave a certain way.
2. The party at fault breached the duty.
3. The breach was the cause in fact of the injuries or damages.
4. The damages were in the scope of the breach.
5. That there were actual damages and injuries caused to you.

If my family lost a loved one as the result of an accident, what legal claims are available?

Louisiana law recognizes two different actions that arise out of a death caused by another person's fault: 1) survival action, and 2) wrongful death action. A survival action permits recovery for those damages suffered by the deceased victim from the time of injury to the moment of his or her death. The elements of damages for a survival action are pain and suffering, loss of earnings, and other damages sustained by the victim up to the moment of death (such as fright, fear, or mental anguish while the deadly ordeal was in progress). A wrongful death action, on the other hand, is intended to compensate surviving family members for their suffering and loss after death. The elements of damage for a wrongful death action are loss of love, affection, companionship, and support, and funeral expenses.

Who can recover damages for wrongful death of a loved one?

It is important to know which family members can recover damages for wrongful death of a loved one. In the event of a death of a family member, only family members closest to the deceased can recover. The law makes an objective decision on which family members are "closest" to the deceased and groups family members into four different categories, which include spouse and children, parents, siblings, and grandparents. The closer family members can recover for wrongful death damages to the exclusion of the others. This means that if someone dies, only those people in the highest-ranking category can recover wrongful death damages. If no one exists or is alive in that category, then people from the next category can make the claim. Any and all people who exist and are living in the category that is the "closest" can make a claim for wrongful death damages.

The categories of family members who can recover for wrongful death damages in order of their priority are:

1. Surviving spouse and/or children of the deceased ("children" includes those who are adopted, legitimate, and illegitimate);
2. Surviving father and/or mother of the deceased, if the deceased left no spouse or child surviving ("parents" includes both biological and adoptive parents);
3. Surviving brothers and/or sisters of the deceased, if the deceased left no spouse, child, or parent surviving ("siblings" include those by half blood, full blood, and adoption); or
4. Surviving grandparents of the deceased, if the deceased left no spouse, child, parent, or sibling surviving.

Neither grandchildren, nor other relatives, are entitled to recover damages for wrongful death, no matter how close they may have been to the deceased.

What damages am I eligible to receive in my car accident injury case?

It is important to understand that your damages are not limited to physical injury. In addition to physical bodily injury, damages can encompass almost any loss that resulted from the accident, such as destruction to one's vehicle, lost wages for the time a person could not work, past and future medical expenses, and sometimes trauma caused by a person's pain and suffering. The most common damages recovered after an auto accident are:

- Property damage
- Medical expenses
- Bodily injury
- Lost wages
- Impaired earning capacity
- Pain and suffering
- Loss of enjoyment of life
- Wrongful death

What property damages does the at-fault driver's insurance company owe me for my damaged vehicle?

Determining the actual amount awarded for property damage depends on whether or not the property was destroyed, if it is repairable, and if there was a loss of use of the property for any period of time. The normal value of recoverable property damage is the "fair market value" of the property if it was totally destroyed, or its decrease in value if it was partially destroyed. The fair market value for a vehicle that is totally destroyed or so badly damaged the cost of repair exceeds its value (*i.e.*, "totaled"), is the value of the vehicle prior to the accident minus its salvage value. On the other hand, if the property can be repaired, then damages are measured by the cost to repair or restore the property. Alternatively, fair market value can be calculated by taking the difference between the value of the vehicle, or other property, before and after the accident occurred. Usually whichever figure is greater and in the injured party's best interest is the one used to determine the amount of damages. Here are some types of costs that can be part of a property damage award:

- Damage to personal belongings caused by the accident
- Towing costs
- Vehicle storage fees
- Appraisals, if necessary
- Public or private property damaged by the accident
- Rental car costs
- Body shop repairs
- Replacement costs

What personal injury damages does the at-fault driver's insurance company owe me for my bodily injuries?

Below are some of the different types of personal injury damages include:

- Past medical expenses
- Ambulance services
- Emergency room visits
- Physical aids and appliances

- Physical therapy
- Doctor visits
- Medical specialists
- Hospital stays
- Transportation costs to and from medical care
- Medication
- Future medical expenses
- Past lost wages
- Future lost wages
- Impaired earning capacity
- Pain and suffering
- Loss of enjoyment of life

Can I recover damages for injuries that existed before my motor vehicle accident?

In general, pre-existing injuries that are not the result of the accident are not recoverable. However, if an earlier injury was aggravated or worsened as a direct result of the accident, then you can recover the medical costs associated with the aggravation of your pre-existing injuries. In short, the insurance company for the driver at fault would owe you for any increased or prolonged pain, but not for the underlying pre-existing condition.

If I miss work because of the accident, can I recover lost wages from the responsible driver's insurance company?

Yes. If you were employed at the time of your accident, you are entitled to recover damages for the wages, commissions, bonuses, tips, etc., you are unable to collect because of absence from your job due to injury. The amount of your lost wages does not need to be proven to a mathematical certainty, but must be well established by the evidence. The following evidence can be used to establish the amount of lost wages you are entitled to recover:

- Statements by employers
- Payroll records
- W-2s
- Tax returns
- Pay stubs
- Social Security records

In addition to lost past wages, you can also recover for the loss of earning capacity and future wages. Some factors to consider that determine the amount of damages for lost future wages include:

- Age of the injured person
- Life expectancy
- Work life expectancy
- Investment income factor
- Productivity increase
- Prospects for rehabilitation
- Future earning capacity
- Loss of future earning capacity
- Loss of earning ability
- Inflation

Are my personal injury claims for pain and suffering compensable?

Yes. You are entitled to seek compensation for the pain and suffering you will endure as a result of your injury. This is generally the component of the personal injury claim that has the greatest value. The amount of damages that can be obtained depends on the severity and duration of the injured person's pain and suffering. There are several types of ailments someone can suffer from (besides physical pain) that can be a considered a component of pain and suffering. Some aspects included in pain and suffering, besides physical discomfort and trauma, are:

- Fright
- Nervousness
- Grief
- Anxiety
- Shock
- Humiliation
- Apprehension
- Mental anguish

In order to recover for this type of damages, the different aspects of your pain and suffering—such as the location, frequency, nature, and type of suffering—must be specifically shown. Ideally, you will be able to describe the nature (sharp, dull, aching, cramping), length (constant, intermittent), aggravating conditions (weather, particular movements, fatigue), and objective symptoms (headaches, nausea, insomnia, limping), if any. Since legal cases often move slowly, it is a good idea to keep a diary of the pain and suffering endured in case you recover and do not remember the details of your injury.

How does my loss of enjoyment of life claim differ from my pain and suffering claim?

Damages for loss of enjoyment of life are similar to pain and suffering, but instead they are awarded for a person's inability to engage in pleasurable activities as a result of the injury sustained. The distinction between the two is that with loss of enjoyment of life something is taken away from the victim, as opposed to the suffering from physical pain or mental anguish. In order to recover for this type of damages, you would have to show that the injury was more than a mere inconvenience. The condition would likely need to be permanent and irreversible, and the loss would have to constitute an important part of your life.

Can my family members make claims for my accident-related injuries?

Select members of your family can make a loss of consortium claim for the way your injuries negatively impacted their lives. A loss of consortium claim allows your family members to be awarded money for the harm and extra burden your accident caused them. Your accident and the injuries you sustained may have caused you to miss spending quality time with your family, you might have been unable to provide financially for a period of time, or perhaps you were unable to do simple household chores like cut the grass. All of these harms and burdens that your accident caused your family to experience are compensable in the same way that you are going to be awarded money for your personal pain and suffering.

A loss of consortium claim can be brought if your family experiences one or more of the following elements:

- Loss of love and affection
- Loss of society and companionship
- Impairment of sexual relations
- Loss of performance of material services
- Loss of financial support
- Loss of aid and assistance
- Loss of fidelity

The following people can bring a loss of consortium claim for damages they sustained from your automobile accident:

- Your spouse
- Your child or children
- Your mother and father
- Your brothers and sisters
- Your grandfather and grandmother.

This list is limited. Fortunately, it does include adoptive relationships.

What types of non-death injury claims are most valuable?

Recoveries vary and each case is different. Nevertheless, the nature of your injury has a major impact on the value of your claims. For example, in general, spinal injuries are worth more than arm, leg, or shoulder problems. Brain injuries are usually more valuable than even neck and back injuries. Severe burn cases are also very valuable.

Permanent nerve damage injuries, like herniated discs in the spine, typically bring larger settlements or judgments than broken bones that will eventually heal (even a fractured spine!) or soft-tissue muscular injuries. Surgical injuries are worth far more than non-surgical harm. Ultimately, the value of your case depends on a variety of factors, including (but not limited to) your future medical needs.

What injuries are most common with car accidents?

Spine injuries of the back and neck are by far the most common cause of accident-related pain and suffering. They occur most frequently in the lower back, also known as the lumbar spine, and the neck, called the cervical spine. Less often, accident-related spine pain arises in middle back (thoracic spine) or the tailbone (sacral spine). Traumatic injury symptoms typically originate from the following anatomic structures in and around the spine:

- Muscles
- Nerves
- Discs
- Joints
- Bones

It is often difficult to diagnose the exact location of the pain source because symptoms arising from different spinal tissues can feel extremely similar. Therefore, it is a challenge to differentiate the potential pain sources without using interventional diagnostic procedures. The problem that uncertain pain source diagnosis presents for injured accident victims is that the confusion clouds the issue of whether the accident or a pre-existing condition caused their injuries. Determining the type of spine tissue causing your pain could help you prove your case against the other driver's insurance company.

Should I expect my accident-related neck or back pain to go away soon?

No. To predict how long your neck or back injury will last, you would need know the location and severity of the exact source of your pain. This is virtually impossible without advanced diagnostic testing like MRI. (X-rays are not good enough!) It is difficult to pinpoint exactly where, anatomically, you are injured or what, diagnostically, is wrong. Some injuries result in a delayed impact. They cause pain long after the accident. The anatomical source of the pain is not always clear.

In the early stages of a spine injury (pre-MRI), it is extraordinarily difficult to determine whether you suffer from a temporary soft-tissue injury or a permanent disc nerve damage injury. You should **never** assume that a neck or back injury is minor and temporary until your doctor and advanced imaging like MRI (not X-rays) confirm the absence of a spinal disc nerve injury.

Should I be concerned if my accident caused headaches, memory loss, confusion, etc.?

Yes. If you experience any of these symptoms following your accident, report them to a doctor ASAP. Car accidents often cause traumatic brain injuries (TBI). TBIs, also known as intracranial injuries, are head injuries that can vary in severity from a mild concussion to severe brain damage. When the brain is jarred or shaken in a car wreck, the impact can cause bruising, swelling, or tearing of the brain tissue. TBI symptoms include unconsciousness, headaches, dizziness, sadness, anger, confusion, trouble concentrating, memory loss, nausea, vomiting, fatigue, drowsiness, and seizures. These problems can be temporary or permanent. TBIs are extraordinarily difficult to diagnose and prove. If you or someone who cares about you noticed any head injury symptoms since your accident, please bring a loved one who knows you well with you to the doctor. Often a spouse, parent, or significant other will be able to report changes and symptoms you cannot notice or remember.

What type of doctor should I see after my motor vehicle accident?

While it is essential to your case that you seek medical attention from a licensed doctor as soon as possible after your accident, the choice of which type of doctor to see is yours. As long as your doctor is qualified to diagnose and treat your injuries, you should be fine.

Below are a few health care provider options to consider:

- Emergency room
- Family practice
- Urgent care
- After-hours clinic
- Neurology
- Orthopedics
- Pain management
- Rheumatology
- Radiology
- Chiropractor
- Physical therapy
- Occupational therapy
- Mental health care
- Other licensed health care provider

Should I go to the emergency room after an accident?

You must consider the urgency of your situation before you decide whether to go to the emergency room (ER) immediately after the accident. If you begin experiencing pain at the scene of the accident, especially severe pain, a trip to the ER is probably a good idea. If your pain is extreme or you are disoriented or confused, you should consider allowing an ambulance to transport you to the ER. The ER can check your vital signs and take X-rays to rule out broken bones. However, in most instances the ER will not order an MRI, so they will be unable to determine whether you have a disc injury in your neck or back. Usually, at the time of discharge the ER will provide instructions to follow up with your primary care physician and other specialists as required. The upside of an ER visit is that it is a great precautionary measure to treat or rule out urgent acute injuries; the downside is that ER bills are extraordinarily expensive.

If you elect to forgo the ER, you should nevertheless see a doctor as soon as any pain or other symptoms arise. If you have a primary care or family doctor, that is typically the best place to start, assuming you can schedule a prompt appointment. Another decent starting point would be an urgent care center or an after-hours clinic.

Whether you began your medical treatment at the ER, family doctor, or after-hours clinic, you should consider seeing a specialist if your symptoms persist more than a few weeks after the accident.

How should I handle my doctor appointments?

It is essential to your personal injury case that your doctors and other health care providers report all your injuries and symptoms caused or aggravated by the motor vehicle accident. Complete and accurate doctor reports are crucial to the successful handling of your bodily injury claims. Ideally, your doctors' reports will 1) set forth all of your injuries and symptoms; 2) describe your pain and suffering; 3) relate your injuries, symptoms, and treatment to the accident; and 4) express an opinion on any related future problems, treatment, restrictions, and disability.

Below is a list of eleven mistakes to avoid when dealing with your doctors:

1. Failure to promptly seek medical attention after the accident.
2. Failure to provide your doctor with a complete and accurate medical history.
3. Missed medical appointments.
4. Failure to describe your pain and symptoms.
5. Failure to inform your doctor that your injury has affected your ability to work.
6. Failure to tell your doctor the truth.
7. Failure to use medication, equipment, or therapy as prescribed.
8. Failure to discuss accident-related depression and anxiety.
9. Failure to take notes and keep a diary of your symptoms and treatment.
10. Ending medical treatment too soon.
11. Discussing your lawsuit with your doctor.

What is an IME?

An IME is a tool that your opponent can use to challenge the diagnoses or opinions of your treating doctor. To do this, they will ask you to submit to evaluation by a doctor hired by the defendant insurance company, which is called an Independent Medical Examination (IME). The IME is actually not entirely "independent" because the IME doctor is usually chosen by the insurance company. This examination will generally involve the injuries that you sustained in the automobile accident. The doctor then provides diagnoses and opinions about your condition. As expected, these will often counter those of your doctor.

If a company employee causes my accident, does his or her company owe me for my damages?

Typically, if you were in an auto accident with an individual while he or she was on the job, that person's employer could be responsible for damages related to your accident. The extent of the employer's responsibility can be determined by keeping a few simple factors in mind.

To know if the employer was responsible for the actions of its employee at the time an auto accident occurred, one has to consider two important factors that determine if this law applies. The first is simply whether an employment relationship existed between the employer and employee. The second is whether the employee's driving of a motor vehicle at the time of the accident was within the scope of that person's employment.

Why are 18-wheeler accidents different than other motor vehicle accidents?

Accidents involving 18-wheelers and other big rigs can differ from the run-of-the-mill motor vehicle accidents. A typical fully-loaded commercial truck, like an 18-wheeler or dump truck, can weigh 25 times as much as a typical car. Although 18-wheeler trucks, tractor semi-trailer vehicles, and other commercial trucks account for only 3–4% of all traffic on the roads in Louisiana, they are involved in about 9% of the total fatalities resulting from auto accidents.

Commercial truck drivers are regulated by the U.S. Department of Transportation, and they have a higher standard of duty and care than non-commercial drivers because of the excessive danger involved with their accidents. Some of the regulations include how much weight a big rig can haul; how long a driver can go without rest; and quality standards, which regulate the manufacturing and repair of commercial trucks. Some of the special rules that apply to 18-wheelers involve driver background checks, drug testing, driver logs, and hours of service, all of which can impact the outcome of a case.

State and federal regulations mandate higher insurance requirements on owners and drivers of large commercial trucks, as compared to regular personal-use vehicles.

Can I trust my lawyer to keep our conversations confidential?

The answer, in a word, is "yes." While clients often value attorneys for qualities such as aggressiveness, intelligence, and creativity, loyalty is our profession's most essential attribute. Through the concept of attorney-client privilege, lawyers are required to keep client communications confidential and they are protected from being forced to reveal client secrets. Attorney-client privilege applies even after a lawyer no longer represents you. Attorneys who breach the privilege can be reprimanded or even disbarred. Airing clients' dirty laundry is considered a breach of fiduciary duty. Therefore, feel free to trust your lawyer to keep your conversations confidential. The attorney-client privilege will protect your privacy.

How long will my case last?

Predicting the length of litigation is difficult. Each case is unique. A host of factors outside your control could expedite or delay the process. Some cases settle quickly, while others last for years awaiting trial and appeals. Usually your attorney will spend months attempting to settle your case before filing a lawsuit. Once litigation is filed, lawyers will conduct pre-trial discovery, an investigatory process that could take years to complete. It begins with formal written requests for information and evidence, followed by depositions where attorneys question witnesses under oath before court reporters. Another common pre-trial activity is mediation, a meeting between the parties and a neutral mediator designed to facilitate a final settlement.

Although some cases settle within weeks, and others last many years, we find that most personal injury cases settle between 6 and 18 months from the time of the accident.

Should I try to settle my case by mediation?

If you would prefer to settle your case for a fair market value sooner rather than taking your chances at trial later, mediation is a good idea. Mediation is a form of Alternative Dispute Resolution (ADR), a general term encompassing various techniques for resolving conflict outside of court using a neutral third party.

In our experience, mediation has a high success rate at settling car accident personal injury claims. Therefore, there is little harm in attempting mediation when the parties believe that an agreement between them could be possible. The following are some of the advantages to be aware of:

- Mediation can help protect privacy since it is a confidential process, unlike courtroom proceedings that are open to the public.
- If the parties agree to settle, the injured party will usually get

the funds within a few weeks as opposed to several months or even years later.
- The parties involved make the decision (not a third person such as a judge or jury), which gives those parties more control over the outcome.
- Having a case decided in mediation may mean lower attorney fees and costs.
- The parties can avoid the stress and uncertainty involved in a drawn-out lawsuit that may take years to resolve.
- If an agreement is not reached in mediation, the case can still be decided by a jury or resolved in some other way.
- Even if parties decide not to settle the case, what happened and was said during mediation is confidential and cannot be brought in court.

What does it mean that someone has a lien against my personal injury settlement?

A lien is a security right placed on personal property to satisfy debt owed to a third person or entity. In the context of your personal injury award, the personal property in question is the settlement money received from the insurance company, or at least the portion that the lien holder is asserting a right to recover.

The most common type of lien in a personal injury case is a medical lien. In many cases, for example, the injured party may not have any health insurance or his or her health insurance does not cover all medical bills. If this is the case, health care providers will seek to recover all their unpaid medicals bills with a lien against the awarded amount. In other words, a personal injury award will likely be reduced by the amount owed for unpaid medical bills related to the auto accident. Although there are other types of liens that can affect the awarded amount, this type of medical lien is the most common.

Even if an insurance company has paid all of your medical bills, other entities may still have a claim to at least a portion of your personal injury award. When an insurance company or other entity pays medical expenses on behalf of an injured person, the company or entity likely has a claim to be reimbursed for the payments they made. The heart of this issue is that you are generally not allowed to "double recover" for medical expenses by both having an insurance company and the at-fault party reimbursing you for your medical bills.

Some types of related statutory and contractual claims to look out for are the following:

- Medicare/Medicaid
- ERISA health insurance plans
- Veterans Administration
- Hospitals
- Workers' compensation
- Medical pay under auto insurance
- Health insurance
- Individual medical providers
- X-ray service providers
- Ambulance
- Chiropractors
- Prior attorneys

An attorney who understands the applicable laws can negotiate your liens and help you put more money in your pocket.

Are personal injury settlements a good or bad thing?

Although unreasonable lowball offers designed to prey upon accident injury victims' financial desperation are bad, carefully negotiated settlements for fair market value are generally a good thing. The benefits of settling your case outweigh the risks associated with gambling on a trial. Settlements do not represent "settling for less." Rather, settling just means that you and the defendant have reached an agreement that ends the lawsuit on terms that both of you can live with.

Settling your case outside of court, without a trial and appeals, will result in much faster payment for your damages. Often, cases that fail to settle can take years to get to trial before a judge or jury. These delays can be lengthened for additional years by the appeals process. Some cases that fail to settle do not pay out for decades. A settlement will shorten the recovery time frame. If you have significant bills to pay out of your personal injury case recovery, that's a big deal.

Settlements can also result in more money in your pocket. First, they can do this by removing the risk of a costly loss at trial or low verdict in your favor. Also, settlements save on court costs, such as expert witness fees, that can run thousands of dollars per hour in some instances. Finally, some fee agreements call for your fees to go up if your case reaches a lawsuit, trial, or appeals, so settling before then could possibly save you legal fees as well.

Finally, settlements can reduce your stress by allowing you to control the outcome with a "sure thing" rather than risking it all by "rolling the dice" on the uncertainty of a trial verdict. There are always big risks with trial. Appeals are also risky. Judges and (especially) juries can be quite unpredictable.

Do I need a lawyer to handle my personal injury case? (The answer may surprise you!)

Maybe. Often you need an attorney to maximize your financial recovery and minimize stressful frustrations—but not always.

Many car wreck injury claims can be fairly settled without involving attorneys. For example, minor injuries requiring less than three months' medical treatment with bills less than $3,000 are often settled directly between the accident victim and insurance company. Although I recommend you consult a lawyer to discuss your case (because each case is different and strict legal filing deadlines may apply), I recognize that not every accident victim will do that, especially in very small cases with limited damages.

If your attempts to settle your own injury claims are unsuccessful, you should contact a Louisiana auto accident injury attorney for a consultation within six months or less of your accident date. Involving an experienced lawyer will "level the playing field" between you and the insurance adjusters who negotiate these claims for a living.

Louisiana Lawyer's Oath

Below is the Louisiana Lawyer's Oath. I made this pledge when I became a duly licensed attorney in 2002. Unlike some personal injury lawyers—the ambulance chasers who give this profession a bad name—I respect the solemn nature of this commitment. These are words to live by. You should settle for nothing less from your attorney.

Louisiana Lawyer's Oath:

I SOLEMNLY SWEAR
I will support the Constitution of the United States and the Constitution of the State of Louisiana;
I will maintain the respect due to courts of justice and judicial officers;
I will not counsel or maintain any suit or proceeding which shall appear to me to be unjust nor any defense except such as I believe to be honestly debatable under the law of the land;
I will employ for the purpose of maintaining the causes confided to me such means only as are consistent with truth and honor and will never seek to mislead the judge or jury by any artifice or false statement of fact or law;
I will maintain the confidence and preserve inviolate the secrets of my client and will accept no compensation in connection with a client's business except from the client or with the client's knowledge and approval;
To opposing parties and their counsel, I pledge fairness, integrity, and civility, not only in court, but also in all written and oral communications;

I will abstain from all offensive personality and advance no fact prejudicial to the honor or reputation of a party or witness unless required by the justice of the cause with which I am charged;
I will never reject from any consideration personal to myself the cause of the defenseless or oppressed or delay any person's cause for lucre or malice.
SO HELP ME GOD!

Louisiana Rules of Professional Conduct

Louisiana Rule of Professional Conduct 1.2. Representation

(a) Subject to the provisions of Rule 1.16 and to paragraphs (c) and (d) of this Rule, a lawyer shall abide by a client's decisions concerning the objectives of representation, and, as required by Rule 1.4, shall consult with the client as to the means by which they are to be pursued. A lawyer may take such action on behalf of the client as is impliedly authorized to carry out the representation. A lawyer shall abide by a client's decision whether to settle a matter. In a criminal case, the lawyer shall abide by the client's decision, after consultation with the lawyer, as to a plea to be entered, whether to waive jury trial and whether the client will testify.

(b) A lawyer's representation of a client, including representation by appointment, does not constitute an endorsement of the client's political, religious, economic, social or moral views or activities.

(c) A lawyer may limit the scope of the representation if the limitation is reasonable under the circumstances and the client gives informed consent.

(d) A lawyer shall not counsel a client to engage, or assist a client, in conduct that the lawyer knows is criminal or fraudulent, but a lawyer may discuss the legal consequences of any proposed course of conduct with a client and may counsel or assist a client to make a good faith effort to determine the validity, scope, meaning or application of the law.

Louisiana Rule of Professional Conduct 1.5. Fees

(a) A lawyer shall not make an agreement for, charge, or collect an unreasonable fee or an unreasonable amount for expenses. The factors to be considered in determining the reasonableness of a fee include the following:

(1) the time and labor required, the novelty and difficulty of the questions involved, and the skill requisite to perform the legal service properly;

(2) the likelihood, if apparent to the client, that the acceptance of the particular employment will preclude other employment by the lawyer;

(3) the fee customarily charged in the locality for similar legal services;

(4) the amount involved and the results obtained;

(5) the time limitations imposed by the client or by the circumstances;

(6) the nature and length of the professional relationship with the client;

(7) the experience, reputation, and ability of the lawyer or lawyers performing the services; and

(8) whether the fee is fixed or contingent.

(b) The scope of the representation and the basis or rate of the fee and expenses for which the client will be responsible shall be communicated to the client, preferably in writing, before or within a reasonable time after commencing the representation, except when the lawyer will charge a regularly represented client on the same basis or rate. Any changes in the basis or rate of the fee or expenses shall also be communicated to the client.

(c) A fee may be contingent on the outcome of the matter for which the service is rendered, except in a matter in which a contingent fee is prohibited by Paragraph (d) or other law. A contingent fee agreement shall be in a writing signed by the client. A copy or duplicate original of the executed agreement shall be given to the client at the time of execution of the agreement. The contingency fee agreement shall state the method by which the fee is to be determined, including the percentage or percentages that shall accrue to the lawyer in the event of settlement, trial or appeal; the litigation and other expenses that are to be deducted from the recovery; and whether such expenses are to be deducted before or after the contingent fee is calculated. The agreement must clearly notify the client of any expenses for which the client will be liable whether or not the client is the prevailing party. Upon conclusion of a contingent fee matter, the lawyer shall provide the client with a written statement stating the outcome of the matter and, if there is a recovery, showing the remittance to the client and the method of its determination.

(d) A lawyer shall not enter into an arrangement for, charge, or collect:

(1) any fee in a domestic relations matter, the payment or amount of which is contingent upon the securing of a divorce or upon the amount of alimony or support, or property settlement in lieu thereof; or

(2) a contingent fee for representing a defendant in a criminal case.

(e) A division of fee between lawyers who are not in the same firm may be made only if:

(1) the client agrees in writing to the representation by all of the lawyers involved, and is advised in writing as to the share of the fee that each lawyer will receive;

(2) the total fee is reasonable; and

(3) each lawyer renders meaningful legal services for the client in the matter.

(f) Payment of fees in advance of services shall be subject to the following rules:

(1) When the client pays the lawyer a fee to retain the lawyer's general availability to the client and the fee is not related to a particular representation, the funds become the property of the lawyer when paid and may be placed in the lawyer's operating account.

(2) When the client pays the lawyer all or part of a fixed fee or of a minimum fee for particular representation with services to be rendered in the future, the funds become the property of the lawyer when paid, subject to the provisions of Rule 1.5(f)(5). Such funds need not be placed in the lawyer's trust account, but may be placed in the lawyer's operating account.

(3) When the client pays the lawyer an advance deposit against fees which are to accrue in the future on an hourly or other agreed basis, the funds remain the property of the client and must be placed in the lawyer's trust account. The lawyer may transfer these

funds as fees are earned from the trust account to the operating account, without further authorization from the client for each transfer, but must render a periodic accounting for these funds as is reasonable under the circumstances.

(4) When the client pays the lawyer an advance deposit to be used for costs and expenses, the funds remain the property of the client and must be placed in the lawyer's trust account. The lawyer may expend these funds as costs and expenses accrue, without further authorization from the client for each expenditure, but must render a periodic accounting for these funds as is reasonable under the circumstances.

(5) When the client pays the lawyer a fixed fee, a minimum fee or a fee drawn from an advanced deposit, and a fee dispute arises between the lawyer and the client, either during the course of the representation or at the termination of the representation, the lawyer shall immediately refund to the client the unearned portion of such fee, if any. If the lawyer and the client disagree on the unearned portion of such fee, the lawyer shall immediately refund to the client the amount, if any, that they agree has not been earned, and the lawyer shall deposit into a trust account an amount representing the portion reasonably in dispute. The lawyer shall hold such disputed funds in trust until the dispute is resolved, but the lawyer shall not do so to coerce the client into accepting the lawyer's contentions. As to any fee dispute, the lawyer should suggest a means for prompt resolution such as mediation or arbitration, including arbitration with the Louisiana State Bar Association Fee Dispute Program.

Louisiana Rule of Professional Conduct 1.8. Conflicts of Interest

(a) A lawyer shall not enter into a business transaction with a client or knowingly acquire an ownership, possessory, security or other pecuniary interest adverse to a client unless:

(1) the transaction and terms on which the lawyer acquires the interest are fair and reasonable to the client and are fully disclosed and transmitted in writing in a manner that can be reasonably understood by the client;

(2) the client is advised in writing of the desirability of seeking and is given a reasonable opportunity to seek the advice of independent legal counsel on the transaction; and

(3) the client gives informed consent, in a writing signed by the client, to the essential terms of the transaction and the lawyer's role in the transaction, including whether the lawyer is representing the client in the transaction.

(b) A lawyer shall not use information relating to representation of a client to the disadvantage of the client unless the client gives informed consent, except as permitted or required by these Rules.

(c) A lawyer shall not solicit any substantial gift from a client, including a testamentary gift, or prepare on behalf of a client an instrument giving the lawyer or a person related to the lawyer any substantial gift unless the lawyer or other recipient of the gift, is related to the client. For purposes of this paragraph, related persons include a spouse, child, grandchild, parent, or grandparent.

(d) Prior to the conclusion of representation of a client, a lawyer shall not make or negotiate an agreement giving the lawyer literary or media rights to a portrayal or account based in substantial part on information relating to the representation.

(e) A lawyer shall not provide financial assistance to a client in connection with pending or contemplated litigation, except as follows:

(1) A lawyer may advance court costs and expenses of litigation, the repayment of which may be contingent on the outcome of the matter, provided that the expenses were reasonably incurred. Court costs and expenses of litigation include, but are not necessarily limited to, filing fees; deposition costs; expert witness fees; transcript costs; witness fees; copy costs; photographic, electronic, or digital evidence production; investigation fees; related travel expenses; litigation related medical expenses; and any other case specific expenses directly related to the representation undertaken, including those set out in Rule 1.8(e)(3).

(2) A lawyer representing an indigent client may pay court costs and expenses of litigation on behalf of the client.

(3) Overhead costs of a lawyer's practice which are those not incurred by the lawyer solely for the purposes of a particular representation, shall not be passed on to a client. Overhead costs include, but are not necessarily limited to, office rent, utility costs, charges for local telephone service, office supplies, fixed asset expenses, and ordinary secretarial and staff services.

With the informed consent of the client, the lawyer may charge as recoverable costs such items as computer legal research charges, long distance telephone expenses, postage charges, copying charges, mileage and outside courier service charges, incurred solely for the purposes of the representation undertaken for that client, provided they are charged at the lawyer's actual, invoiced costs for these expenses.

With client consent and where the lawyer's fee is based upon an hourly rate, a reasonable charge for paralegal services may be chargeable to the client. In all other instances, paralegal services shall be considered an overhead cost of the lawyer.

(4) In addition to costs of court and expenses of litigation, a lawyer may provide financial assistance to a client who is in necessitous circumstances, subject however to the following restrictions.

(i) Upon reasonable inquiry, the lawyer must determine that the client's necessitous circumstances, without minimal financial assistance, would adversely affect the client's ability to initiate and/or maintain the cause for which the lawyer's services were engaged.

(ii) The advance or loan guarantee, or the offer thereof, shall not be used as an inducement by the lawyer, or anyone acting on the lawyer's behalf, to secure employment.

(iii) Neither the lawyer nor anyone acting on the lawyer's behalf may offer to make advances or loan guarantees prior to being hired by a client, and the lawyer shall not publicize nor advertise a willingness to make advances or loan guarantees to clients.

(iv) Financial assistance under this rule may provide but shall not exceed that minimum sum necessary to meet the client's, the client's spouse's, and/or dependents' documented obligations for food, shelter, utilities, insurance, non-litigation related medical care and treatment, transportation expenses, education, or other documented expenses necessary for subsistence.

(5) Any financial assistance provided by a lawyer to a client,

whether for court costs, expenses of litigation, or for necessitous circumstances, shall be subject to the following additional restrictions.

(i) Any financial assistance provided directly from the funds of the lawyer to a client shall not bear interest, fees, or charges of any nature.

(ii) Financial assistance provided by a lawyer to a client may be made using a lawyer's line of credit or loans obtained from financial institutions in which the lawyer has no ownership, control and/or security interest; provided, however, that this prohibition shall not apply to any federally insured bank, savings and loan association, savings bank, or credit union where the lawyer's ownership, control and/or security interest is less than 15%. Where the lawyer uses such loans to provide financial assistance to a client, the lawyer should make reasonable, good faith efforts to procure a favorable interest rate for the client.

(iii) Where the lawyer uses a line of credit or loans obtained from financial institutions to provide financial assistance to a client, the lawyer shall not pass on to the client interest charges, including any fees or other charges attendant to such loans, in an amount exceeding the actual charge by the third party lender, or ten percentage points above the bank prime loan rate of interest as reported by the Federal Reserve Board on January 15th of each year in which the loan is outstanding, whichever is less.

(iv) A lawyer providing a guarantee or security on a loan a made in favor of a client may do so only to the extent that the interest charges, including any fees or other charges attendant to such a loan, do not exceed ten percentage points (10%) above the bank prime loan rate of interest as reported by the Federal Reserve Board on January 15th of each year in which the loan is outstanding. Interest together with other charges attendant to such loans which exceeds this maximum may not be the subject of the lawyer's guarantee or security.

(v) The lawyer shall procure the client's written consent to the terms and conditions under which such financial assistance is made. Nothing in this rule shall require client consent in those matters in which a court has certified a class under applicable state or federal law; provided, however, that the court must have accepted and exercised responsibility for making the determination that interest and fees are owed, and that the amount of interest and fees chargeable to the client is fair and reasonable considering the facts and circumstances presented.

(vi) In every instance where the client has been provided financial assistance by the lawyer, the full text of this rule shall be provided to the client at the time of execution of any settlement documents, approval of any disbursement sheet as provided for in Rule 1.5, or upon submission of a bill for the lawyer's services.

(vii) For purposes of Rule 1.8(e), the term "financial institution" shall include a federally insured financial institution and any of its affiliates, bank, savings and loan, credit union, savings bank, loan or finance company, thrift, and any other business or person that, for a commercial purpose, loans or advances money to attorneys and/or the clients of attorneys for court costs, litigation expenses, or for necessitous circumstances.

(f) A lawyer shall not accept compensation for representing a client from one other than the client unless:

(1) the client gives informed consent, or the compensation is provided by contract with a third person such as an insurance contract or a prepaid legal service plan;

(2) there is no interference with the lawyer's independence or professional judgment or with the client-lawyer relationship; and

(3) information relating to representation of a client is protected as required by Rule 1.6.

(g) A lawyer who represents two or more clients shall not participate in making an aggregate settlement of the claims of or against the clients, or in a criminal case an aggregated agreement as to guilty or nolo contendere pleas, unless each client gives informed consent, in a writing signed by the client, or a court approves a settlement in a certified class action. The lawyer's disclosure shall include the existence and nature of all the claims or pleas involved and of the participation of each person in the settlement.

(h) A lawyer shall not:

(1) make an agreement prospectively limiting the lawyer's liability to a client for malpractice unless the client is independently represented in making the agreement; or

(2) settle a claim or potential claim for such liability with an unrepresented client or former client unless that person is advised in writing of the desirability of seeking and is given a reasonable opportunity to seek the advice of independent legal counsel in connection therewith.

(i) A lawyer shall not acquire a proprietary interest in the cause of action or subject matter of litigation the lawyer is conducting for a client, except that the lawyer may:

(1) acquire a lien authorized by law to secure the lawyer's fee or expenses; and

(2) contract with a client for a reasonable contingent fee in a civil case.

(j) [Reserved].

(k) A lawyer shall not solicit or obtain a power of attorney or mandate from a client which would authorize the attorney, without first obtaining the client's informed consent to settle, to enter into a binding settlement agreement on the client's behalf or to execute on behalf of the client any settlement or release documents. An attorney may obtain a client's authorization to endorse and negotiate an instrument given in settlement of the client's claim, but only after the client has approved the settlement.

(l) While lawyers are associated in a firm, a prohibition in the foregoing paragraphs (a) through (k) that applies to any one of them shall apply to all of them.

Louisiana Rule of Professional Conduct 1.15. Safekeeping Property

(a) A lawyer shall hold property of clients or third persons that is in a lawyer's possession in connection with a representation separate from the lawyer's own property. Except as provided in (g) and the IOLTA Rules below, funds shall be kept in one or more separate interest-bearing client trust accounts maintained in a bank or savings and loan association: 1) authorized by federal or state law to do business in Louisiana, the deposits of which are insured by an agency of the federal government; 2) in the state where the lawyer's primary office is situated, if not within Louisiana; or 3) elsewhere with the consent of the client or third person. No earnings on a client trust account may be made available to or utilized by a lawyer or law firm. Other property shall be identified as such and appropriately safeguarded. Complete records of such account funds and other property shall be kept by the lawyer and shall be preserved for a period of five years after termination of the representation.

(b) A lawyer may deposit the lawyer's own funds in a client trust account for the sole purpose of paying bank service charges on that account or obtaining a waiver of those charges, but only in an amount necessary for that purpose.

(c) A lawyer shall deposit into a client trust account legal fees and expenses that have been paid in advance, to be withdrawn by the lawyer only as fees are earned or expenses incurred. The lawyer shall deposit legal fees and expenses into the client trust account consistent with Rule 1.5(f).

(d) Upon receiving funds or other property in which a client or third person has an interest, a lawyer shall promptly notify the client or third person. For purposes of this rule, the third person's interest shall be one of which the lawyer has actual knowledge, and shall be limited to a statutory lien or privilege, a final judgment addressing disposition of those funds or property, or a written agreement by the client or the lawyer on behalf of the client guaranteeing payment out of those funds or property. Except as stated in this rule or otherwise permitted by law or by agreement with the client, a lawyer shall promptly deliver to the client or third person any funds or other property that the client or third person is entitled to receive and, upon request by the client or third person, shall promptly render a full accounting regarding such property.

(e) When in the course of representation a lawyer is in possession of property in which two or more persons (one of whom may be the lawyer) claim interests, the property shall be kept separate by the lawyer until the dispute is resolved. The lawyer shall promptly distribute all portions of the property as to which the interests are not in dispute.

(f) Every check, draft, electronic transfer, or other withdrawal instrument or authorization from a client trust account shall be personally signed by a lawyer or, in the case of electronic, telephone, or wire transfer, from a client trust account, directed by a lawyer or, in the case of a law firm, one or more lawyers authorized by the law firm. A lawyer shall not use any debit card or automated teller machine card to withdraw funds from a client trust account. On client trust accounts, cash withdrawals and checks made payable to "Cash" are prohibited. A lawyer shall subject all client trust accounts to a reconciliation process at least quarterly, and shall maintain records of the reconciliation as mandated by this rule.1

(g) A lawyer shall create and maintain an "IOLTA Account," which is a pooled interest-bearing client trust account for funds of clients or third persons which are nominal in amount or to be held for such a short period of time that the funds would not be expected to earn income for the client or third person in excess of the costs incurred to secure such income.

(1) IOLTA Accounts shall be of a type approved and authorized by the Louisiana Bar Foundation and maintained only in "eligible" financial institutions, as approved and certified by the Louisiana Bar Foundation. The Louisiana Bar Foundation shall establish regulations, subject to approval by the Supreme Court of Louisiana, governing the determination that a financial institution is eligible to hold IOLTA Accounts and shall at least annually publish a list of LBF-approved/certified eligible financial institutions. Participation in the IOLTA program is voluntary for financial institutions.

IOLTA Accounts shall be established at a bank or savings and loan association authorized by federal or state law to do business in Louisiana, the deposits of which are insured by an agency of the federal government or at an open-end investment company registered with the Securities and Exchange Commission authorized by federal or state law to do business in Louisiana which shall be invested solely in or fully collateralized by U.S. Government Securities with total assets of at least $250,000,000 and in order for a financial institution to be approved and certified by the Louisiana Bar Foundation as eligible, shall comply with the following provisions:

(A) No earnings from such an account shall be made available to a lawyer or law firm.

(B) Such account shall include all funds of clients or third persons which are nominal in amount or to be held for such a short period of time the funds would not be expected to earn income for the client or third person in excess of the costs incurred to secure such income.

(C) Funds in each interest-bearing client trust account shall be subject to withdrawal upon request and without delay, except as permitted by law.

(2) To be approved and certified by the Louisiana Bar Foundation as eligible, financial institutions shall maintain IOLTA Accounts which pay an interest rate comparable to the highest interest rate or dividend generally available from the institution to its non-IOLTA customers when IOLTA Accounts meet or exceed the same minimum balance or other eligibility qualifications, if any. In determining the highest interest rate or dividend generally available from the institution to its non-IOLTA accounts, eligible institutions may consider factors, in addition to the IOLTA Account balance, customarily considered by the institution when setting interest rates or dividends for its customers, provided that such factors do not discriminate between IOLTA Accounts and accounts of non-IOLTA customers, and that these factors do not include that the account is an IOLTA Account. The eligible institution shall calculate interest and dividends in accordance with its standard practice for non-IOLTA customers, but the eligible institution may elect to pay a higher interest or dividend rate on IOLTA Accounts.

(3) To be approved and certified by the Louisiana Bar Foundation as eligible, a financial institution may achieve rate comparability required in (g)(2) by:

(A) Establishing the IOLTA Account as: (1) an interest-bearing checking account; (2) a money market deposit account with or tied to checking; (3) a sweep account which is a money market fund or daily (overnight) financial institution repurchase agreement invested solely in or fully collateralized by U.S. Government Securities; or (4) an open-end money market fund solely invested in or fully collateralized by U.S. Government Securities. A daily financial institution repurchase agreement may be established only with an eligible institution that is "well-capitalized" or "adequately capitalized" as those terms are defined by applicable federal statutes and regulations. An open-end money market fund must be invested solely in U.S. Government Securities or repurchase agreements fully collateralized by U.S. Government Securities, must hold itself out as a "money-market fund" as that term is defined by federal statutes and regulations under the Investment Company Act of 1940, and, at the time of the investment, must have total assets of at least $250,000,000. "U.S. Government Securities" refers to U.S. Treasury obligations and obligations issued or guaranteed as to principal and interest by the United States or any agency or instrumentality thereof.

(B) Paying the comparable rate on the IOLTA checking account in lieu of establishing the IOLTA Account as the higher rate product; or

(C) Paying a "benchmark" amount of qualifying funds equal to 60% of the Federal Fund Target Rate as of the first business day of the quarter or other IOLTA remitting period; no fees may be deducted from this amount which is deemed already to be net of "allowable reasonable fees."

(4) Lawyers or law firms depositing the funds of clients or third persons in an IOLTA Account shall direct the depository institution:

(A) To remit interest or dividends, net of any allowable reasonable fees on the average monthly balance in the account, or as otherwise computed in accordance with an eligible institution's standard accounting practice, at least quarterly, to the Louisiana Bar Foundation, Inc.;

(B) to transmit with each remittance to the Foundation, a statement, on a form approved by the LBF, showing the name of the lawyer or law firm for whom the remittance is sent and for each account: the rate of interest or dividend applied; the amount of interest or dividends earned; the types of fees deducted, if any; and the average account balance for each account for each month of the period in which the report is made; and

(C) to transmit to the depositing lawyer or law firm a report in accordance with normal procedures for reporting to its depositors.

(5) "Allowable reasonable fees" for IOLTA Accounts are: per check charges; per deposit charges; a fee in lieu of minimum balance; sweep fees and a reasonable IOLTA Account administrative fee. All other fees are the responsibility of, and may be charged to, the lawyer or law firm maintaining the IOLTA Account. Fees or service charges that are not "allowable reasonable fees" include, but are not limited to: the cost of check printing; deposit stamps; NSF charges; collection charges; wire transfers; and fees for cash management. Fees or charges in excess of the earnings accrued on the account for any month or quarter shall not be taken from earnings accrued on other IOLTA Accounts or from the principal of the account. Eligible financial institutions may elect to waive any or all fees on IOLTA Accounts.

(6) A lawyer is not required independently to determine whether an interest rate is comparable to the highest rate or dividend generally available and shall be in presumptive compliance with Rule 1.15(g) by maintaining a client trust account of the type approved and authorized by the Louisiana Bar Foundation at an "eligible" financial institution.

Acknowledgments

The following people deserve my profound thanks:

- My clients, for trusting me to protect their rights during difficult times;

- My wife, **Brandie Bruno Layrisson**, for supporting me in all that I do;

- My team—**Ashley Richardson, Meghan Notariano, Joe Dunams**, and **Angela Daniel**—for sharing their unique talents and bright ideas;

- My father-in-law, **Nick Bruno**, for reminding me that some accident victims battle injuries for a lifetime;

- **Sherlyne Meissner**, for providing a strong foundation for my education;

- **Cynthia Foster Evans**, for preparing me for college and beyond;

- **Professor Bill Crawford**, for inspiring me with his outstanding teaching, treatise, and example;

- The late **Professor Lee Hargrave**, for guiding me through my first year in legal publishing;

- **Professor Howard L'Enfant**, for injecting humor and empathy into my law school lessons;

- **Professor Frank Maraist**, for educating me about tort law, evidence, and legal writing;

- **Attorney General Richard Ieyoub** and **Mike "Beachball" Russell**, for making my first year as an attorney unforgettable;

- **Judge Stanwood Duval**, for mentoring me with a genuine interest in my career;

- **Andrew Edwards**, for providing an Atticus-like role model of a small-town lawyer;

- The late **Tom Waterman**, for showing me how a true Southern gentleman practices law;

- **Bryan McMahon**, for allowing me to serve *The Ponchatoula Times* as its legal columnist and attorney;

- **Dom Scandurro, Tim Scandurro, Steve Scandurro, Jean-Paul Layrisson,** and **Dewey Scandurro**, for introducing me to personal injury law;

- **Bry Layrisson**, for remaining my best man while protecting our community;

- **Louie Layrisson,** for showing me how the best lawyers at the biggest firms operate;

- **Ben Richardson**, for years of free tech support and a lifetime of unwavering friendship;

- **Wil and Angelique Richardson**, for ensuring that we built a financially successful law firm and always having my back;

- **Chad Richard**, for financing my firm's startup during his banking years;

- **Britt Monteleone**, for answering the call every time I ever needed his help;

- **Steve Parra**, for promoting my practice to friends in need of legal services;

- **Joseph Jones**, for staying in touch and offering his wisdom while traveling the world;

- **Chance Enmon**, for flying me on a private plane to watch the Saints win the Super Bowl (best client gift ever!);

- **Jeff LeSaicherre**, for sharing his insight into how to build a successful law firm;

- **Chad and Samantha Stone**, for supporting my firm since the early years;

- **Marshall Graves**, for keeping our cars running and trusting me to take care of his family;

- **Wesley Daniels**, for helping us find the perfect home office property;

- **Greg Crovetto**, for being the life of the party and the best of many great interns;

- **Erin Brune**, for staying in touch and providing great proofreading in a pinch;

- **Emily Mayeaux**, for carefully editing multiple book manuscripts;

- **Lane Grigas**, for designing great book covers and much more;

- **Tim McHugh**, for sharing his publishing expertise and contacts;

- **Jon Grest, Kenny Bordes, Megan Wiggins,** and **Francis Boustany**, for providing excellent legal research;

- **Robert Barsley, Glen Galbraith, Charlton Meginley, Leta Branch, Lori Stillwell, Jon Yeager,** and **Isaac Zaleski**, for proofreading the manuscript;

- **Chris Zainey**, for reviewing the manuscript and providing great feedback;

- **Robb Campbell,** for working with me on important cases and evaluating the manuscript;

- **John Alford**, for helping me handle personal injury cases I would not want to tackle alone;

- **Ernie Svenson**, for advising me on publishing, marketing, and much more;

- **Gary Boutwell** and **Ravi Sangisetty**, for sharing their considerable knowledge of personal injury law; and

- **Ed Walters, Darrel Papillion,** and **J. Cullens,** for showing me how to handle the really big, complicated personal injury and wrongful death cases the right way.

About The Author

Parker Layrisson helps people injured in car accidents recover the compensation they deserve, without needless frustration and stress, even if they have no money to pay him or their doctors. He does that by forcing giant insurance companies to play by the rules when dealing with regular people like you.

Mr. Layrisson is an experienced attorney and published author with law offices located in New Orleans and Ponchatoula, Louisiana. He is a former federal judicial law clerk, state assistant attorney general, parish special counsel, and city prosecutor who served as editor-in-chief of the *Louisiana Law Review*. He has received Martindale-Hubbell's highest peer review rating for professional excellence in legal abilities and ethical standards (AV Preeminent) and Avvo®'s highest available rating (10/10 Superb). He also earned the Lexis Nexis® Lawyers.com Client Distinction Award and the Avvo® Client Choice Award. He was named to *New Orleans Magazine*'s list of "Top Lawyers" in 2009 and *Louisiana Super Lawyers*' "Rising Stars" list since 2012.

Mr. Layrisson graduated with honors from Tulane University and LSU Law Center. He is a former No. 1 ranked law student and a member of the Order of the Coif (top 10% of graduates). He has taught law, professionalism, and ethics to attorneys and judges in various continuing legal education courses.

Mr. Layrisson is Past President of the 21st Judicial District Young Lawyers Association, Port Manchac, and the Ponchatoula Rotary Club. He has also served as a member of the LSU Law Chancellor's Council and Vice President and Treasurer of SAFE (f/k/a the Southeast Spouse Abuse Program). He has written numerous law books, reports, and newspaper columns, and maintains a blog at www.Layrisson.com.

Parker Layrisson is married to Brandie Bruno Layrisson. They live in Ponchatoula.

Why We're Different

The Parker Layrisson Law Firm is not a general law practice open to accepting all types of cases. We do not handle every area of law. Instead of spreading our resources among a wide variety of practice areas, we focus our attention on helping people injured in car accidents recover the compensation they deserve, without needless frustration and stress—even if they have no money to pay us or their doctors.

Auto accident personal injury law is our passion. It is what we do. We limit our caseload to serious injury and wrongful death matters, and that is good for you.

> **FAST FACT**
> Every member of our team has been involved in an automobile accident.

Every member of our team has been involved in an automobile accident. Three of us were seriously injured as a result of a car crash. We have personally experienced the stress and financial pressure caused by accidents with injuries.

That is why we work hard to "go the extra mile" for our clients. Whether it's providing a satellite office in downtown New Orleans for client convenience, investing in state-of-the-art technology, or contacting our current and former clients every month with free legal tips, we go above and beyond expectations to provide incredible value to the people who trust us to protect their rights.

The Parker Layrisson Law Firm differs from other auto accident firms in that we do not rely on a high-volume bulk practice. We do not advertise on TV, over radio, or in the Yellow Pages. Nearly 90% of our cases come by referrals from former clients, doctors, judges, attorneys, and other contacts throughout our community who trust us to help accident victims based on our unique experience, qualifications, and reputation.

We are not a "chop-shop" or "mill" that turns over hundreds of injury cases every year. In fact, we decline more cases than we accept. We value quality over quantity in our caseload, and we look for clients who do the same when choosing an attorney. We want the best clients around, not the most cases.

By handling fewer cases and focusing on auto accident personal injury, we can allocate more resources to your case. If the Parker Layrisson Law Firm accepts your case, our experienced team will handle your matter from start to finish. We will not palm you off to inexperienced assistants or associates. We will dedicate extensive resources to your case, and it will show.

Our team delivers excellent client care by aggressively representing injury victims and keeping them informed with prompt, thorough communications. At all times, our law firm maintains the highest standards of professional excellence and ethics. Our team includes an experienced auto accident attorney and professional support staff.

> **FAST FACT**
> Nearly 90% of our cases come by referrals from former clients, doctors, judges, attorneys, and others who trust us to help.

Our focus is simple but important: helping people injured in car accidents recover the compensation they deserve—with less stress!

Instead of badgering potential clients with high-pressure sales techniques and "your pain is my gain" advertising, we offer accident victims free information you can review in the privacy of your home, at your own pace, by providing free consumer guides, newsletters, articles, and other resources via mail and the internet. We prefer clients who are as careful in their selection process as we are.

> **FAST FACT**
> We offer you free information you can review in the privacy of your home, at your own pace: books, newsletters, videos, etc.

Most importantly, we focus on the "relationship" part of the attorney-client relationship. That means we don't drop clients when their case ends and ignore them forever after. Rather, we stay in touch, and we continue to offer them value through our free VIP program, which provides frequent legal tips, newsletters packed with helpful information, and much more. Relationships require hard work, commitment, and patience. Our clients deserve nothing less.

Cases We Do Not Accept

Due to the high volume of calls from potential clients, including referrals from former clients and other attorneys that our law firm receives, we have found that the only way to provide exceptional personal service to the clients we accept is to decline those cases that do not meet our strict selection criteria. Therefore, we generally do not accept the following types of cases:

> **FAST FACT**
> We decline more cases than we accept.

- Cases that focus on issues other than car accident personal injury and wrongful death, such as divorces, child custody disputes, employment discrimination, criminal defense, business litigation, transactional matters, real estate title, estate planning, civil rights, etc.

- Cases with automobile accidents resulting in property damage but no injuries.

- Cases with no medical evidence of injury (*i.e.*, those in which there are no visits to the doctor). Sorry, but if you have not been treated or will not treat with a health care provider who can verify that you were injured by the accident, then we will not accept your case. Insurance companies don't pay much for cases without objective evidence of injury. There may be plenty of lawyers who take those cases, but we do not.

- Cases with less than $3,000 in "hard damages." Your case must have at least $3,000 in past and future medical bills before we will consider accepting it. We would like to represent everyone who needs a good attorney, but we cannot. If you have a question about whether your future medicals will likely reach $3,000, contact us and we can help you figure it out.

- Cases where the one-year prescriptive period (*i.e.*, statute of limitations) will soon run out. We require at least three months to adequately investigate and evaluate your claim before the prescriptive deadline arrives, so we only consult with potential clients within nine months of the accident.

- Cases involving people who have had several accident claims in the near past. Many jurors and some judges tend to look dimly on claimants who have a significant accident history. It may not be fair, but it's a reality, so we avoid representing "frequent filers."

- Cases where the police who investigated the accident charged you. We know that the police can be wrong; but if, after interviewing the witnesses and evaluating the scene of the accident, the policeman gave you and not the other driver a ticket, then we typically will not represent you.

- Cases where you were at fault in the accident. If there is any substantial evidence that your injury is in any way your fault, then we will not accept your case.

- Cases where another attorney has already filed your claim or lawsuit. At the Parker Layrisson Law Firm, we handle cases our own way. If another lawyer has already filed your claim or lawsuit, that's fine, but it means we will not handle the matter. We handle cases from beginning to end, rather than take over midway through the process for other lawyers. Please choose us first, or not at all.

Cases We Do Accept

If you can answer "yes" to the following six questions, we may be the right auto accident personal injury law firm for you:

1. Was the accident someone else's fault?
2. Was there visible property damage to your vehicle?
3. Did you get (or will you get) medical treatment shortly after the accident?

4. Have you followed your doctor's treatment recommendations?
5. Did the accident happen less than 9 months ago?
6. Is there insurance available to cover your damages?

If you answered "yes" to all of those questions, and you would like to learn more about your legal options, contact Parker Layrisson today:

New Orleans: 504-264-1515*
Ponchatoula: 985-467-9525
*By Appointment

www.Layrisson.com

Rave Reviews from Our Clients

"I would recommend Parker Layrisson Law Firm to anyone wanting a 'no-hassle situation.' They kept me informed throughout the entire case, and it was resolved quickly. I was very satisfied."
Demetrius Carter – Ponchatoula, LA

"I wanted my life back, but I wasn't getting anywhere on my own. I couldn't have found a better lawyer. Parker and his team took care of everything for me. He was smart, dedicated, and believed in me every step of the way."
Myra Deliberto – Hammond, LA

"I know I can count on Parker when I have a legal issue. He takes care of my questions quickly so I can take care of my business. And most importantly, he took care of my family when we needed it. I would recommend him to anyone needing to protect the ones they love."
Marshall Graves – Baton Rouge, LA

"I'm proud to be a Parker Layrisson Law Firm client. Parker and Angela do a great job protecting my rights, keeping me informed, and treating me with utmost respect. I would recommend them to anyone in need of excellent accident injury attorneys."
Debra Hills – Ponchatoula, LA

"Parker is an excellent lawyer. His team did a wonderful job for our family. We are very satisfied and highly recommend the firm."
Jeffery LaMarca – Hammond, LA

"After taking care of my accident case, Parker has continued to help me out through the years with any legal questions I have. I tell my friends and family to call Parker—he's great! And if he can't help you, he can help you find someone who can."
Shawna Martin – Kenner, LA

"When I was injured in a car accident, I just wanted to get back to my life and business as quickly as possible. The team at Parker Layrisson Law Firm was professional, helpful, and took care of everything."
Bryan Poche – Ponchatoula, LA

"As soon as I hired Parker, I knew I was in good hands. I was confident that he would work hard to get me the best possible medical treatment and overall outcome for my injuries. The professionalism displayed by him and his staff assured me that I had called the right attorney!"
Somiya Thomas – Ponchatoula, LA

"Parker and his staff were great, caring, and truly concerned. I was treated like family."
Linda Thevenot – Ponchatoula, LA

"After our wreck, the insurance companies were giving us the run around. My pain was getting worse, and someone recommended Parker. He was very helpful and informative. He is also easily accessible. He is easy to talk to and he will take care of you."
Bronwyn Bankston – Ponchatoula, LA

"I was worried I would not know what was going on, but everyone informed me of each step and made me feel more comfortable about the situation. Parker showed me that he would be up front and honest about everything."
Anthony Provence, Jr. – Hammond, LA

"Parker kept me involved and took care of everything I needed. They did an amazing job. They have a great team."
Steven Lucia – Laplace, LA

"Mr. Layrisson was on point with everything that was involved with the case. I HIGHLY recommend Parker Layrisson to anybody."
Paul Loyacano III – Hammond, LA

"Parker was always quick to respond to all questions and concerns. He was always up front and he never gave false expectations. He answered all questions with honesty."
James Sanders – Manchac, LA

"I liked everything about Parker Layrisson Law Firm's service. They are a good team to work with and very honest about their work. I would recommend them to others."
Kadarrel Brooks – Ponchatoula, LA

"I liked the constant contact and updates on the progress of the case. Everything from my point of view was incredibly easy. This is an excellent law office. Parker is a highly respected member of our community."
Jason Anderson – Ponchatoula, LA

Testimonials from Other Attorneys

"You can trust Parker Layrisson with your personal injury case. I know that because I have personally worked with Parker on numerous cases. I have seen how he conducts himself 'behind the scenes.' Parker is hardworking, ethical, and compassionate. He knows car accident law inside and out, and he is not afraid to stand up to big insurance companies."

John S. Alford
Attorney at Law – Covington, LA

"I have worked with Parker on numerous cases all over Louisiana. He is exceptionally smart and always well-prepared. The one thing that has always impressed me about Parker is his candor and empathy towards his clients. He has always been very detailed in his analysis of the cases upfront with the clients, ensuring that there are no surprises down the road. Parker is a master at making difficult legal issues easy to understand. Clients need compassion from their advocate, and Parker is there for them when they need him."

Robert L. Campbell
Attorney at Law – Baton Rouge, LA

"I've worked with Parker Layrisson in numerous cases, including seeing him in action at trial. Parker is sharp, tough, and aggressive. He works hard for his clients."

Steven M. Gonzalez
Attorney at Law – New Orleans, LA

"Parker is dedicated to his clients and he takes a detailed approach. We have worked together on legal cases and even co-authored a law book, so I have closely watched his progress for years. Parker practices law with skill and integrity. If you need a personal injury lawyer in the Ponchatoula-Hammond area, I highly recommend Parker Layrisson."

Robert J. Landry
Attorney at Law – Houma, LA

"Parker Layrisson is without question one of the most intelligent, successful, and professional attorneys in Tangipahoa Parish, if not the entire state of Louisiana. Over the years, I have referred dozens of my clients, friends, and family members to Parker. He has earned my trust by handling their personal injury cases with great skill and personal attention every time."

Jeff A. LeSaicherre
Attorney at Law – Hammond, LA

"As a fellow attorney, colleague, and trusted friend, I routinely reach out to Parker for advice and to discuss wide ranging legal issues that come up in the every day practice of law. Parker is not only one of the brightest legal minds in our community, but perhaps more importantly, he is a caring and devoted advocate for those who are not always able to speak for themselves."

J. Christopher Zainey, Jr.
Attorney at Law – New Orleans, LA

Contact Information

Parker Layrisson
Attorney at Law

Parker Layrisson Law Firm
200 East Hickory Street
Ponchatoula, LA 70454

985-467-9525

www.Layrisson.com

Join the VIP List

Legal challenges are complex, and they can often be overwhelming. One of our missions at the Parker Layrisson Law Firm is to inform and educate our clients and other VIPs about the law, before they need the knowledge, so that they are well prepared to face legal challenges when they arise. We invite you to apply for VIP Membership by signing up online at www.LawFirmVIP.com or calling us at 985-467-9525.

VIP List Exclusive Membership Benefits:

- Legal Education That Empowers You—At No Cost!
- Personal Relationships with Our Team
- Monthly Legal Tips by Postcard
- Subscription to Layrisson Law Letter
- VIP Access to Lawyer Referral Recommendations
- More Helpful Information by Mail and Email
- Never More Than a Few Emails per Month
- We Never Share Your Info with Others (NO SPAM!)
- Fun VIP ONLY Giveaways
- 10% Discount on Legal Fees

BECOME A VIP FOR FREE!
www.LawFirmVIP.com